# The Tea Garden

# 茶庭

大橋治三 写真集

Each photo caption is described as follows :
*Ginkaku-ji Togu-do A Complete View Muromachi Era Kyoto*
Title     Item                        Time          Place

*The Tea Garden*
*Copyright © 1989 Graphic-sha Publishing Co., Ltd.*
*1-9-12 Kudankita, Chiyoda-ku, Tokyo 102, Japan*
*ISBN4-7661-0543-5*

*Printed in Japan*

*First Printing, 1989*

# 茶庭

大橋治三
写真集

# 目次　　Contents

# 露地のこころ　　　千　宗室（裏千家家元）

『南方録』の冒頭に、利休居士は茶の湯とはなにかということについて、次のように記しています。

　　家ハもらぬほど、食事ハ飢ぬほどにてたる事也、是仏の教、茶の湯の本意也、水を運び、薪をとり、湯をわ
　　かし、茶をたてて、仏にそなへ、人にもほどこし、吾ものむ、花をたて香をたく、ミなミな仏祖の行ひのあ
　　とを学ぶ也

居士はまず知足安分、すなわち「足るを知る」ということを教えています。足るを知るとは分相応に満足する
ということです。足るを知ってはじめて、自らの労力で火をおこし、水を汲み、湯を沸かして茶を点てるわけで
す。こうして点てた茶は、まず「仏に供え」「人にも与え」、そして最後に「我も飲む」のです。これが茶の湯の
基本姿勢です。一盌の茶を捧げる意味がここにあります。

利休居士は同じく『南方録』の中に、「わびは清浄無垢の仏世界をあらわす」ともいっております。茶の湯とは
宗教の実践の場だというわけです。茶の湯が宗教の実践の場として成立するために、現象面で必要となったのが
露地でありました。

茶の庭のことを通常〝露地〟というのですが、露地とは仏教的な解釈では、「あらわ」ということで、すべてを
あらわにするということです。それも単に「目にあらわ」という意ではなく、「心も身もあらわにする」というこ
とです。すべてをさらけ出すという意味です。

茶会を催す亭主は、客が通る道路である露地をみずからが清掃して、打水をします。亭主はまず、心の中のこ
だわりや煩悩などは捨て去り、洗い清めなければなりません。

客も露地を通って蹲踞で手と口を清めます。単に洗うのではありません。そのとき、客の心境は、「身心是露浄」
でなくてはなりません。身心ともに一片の汚れもなく清浄であるという意です。客は蹲踞で手と口を清めたあと、
躙口から席入りするとき、自分の履物を始末します。ところがせっかく清めた手で履物を扱うというのは矛盾し
ているのではないかと疑問を口にする人がいます。それはまったく露地の本質を知らないための質問なのです。
露地は汚れた場ではありません。亭主自らが心をこめて打水し、雑巾で飛び石を拭き清め、あたりの木々にもた
っぷりと水を掛け、すべてを清浄にととのえた特別の道であって、

　　「三界の火宅を出て白露地に住する」

という娑婆世界から画然と切り離されたすばらしい別天地であるということを思うべきです。露地を歩いてきた
から、その履物を扱うのは汚いといってしまったら、それこそどこへも行けなくなってしまいます。

茶席の躙口から入る前に、蹲踞で手と口を清める行為は、キリスト教の聖堂に入ったときに聖水で身を清める
行為と同じです。蹲踞の水はまさにホーリー・ウォーター（聖水）にほかなりません。神社仏閣の参詣用手水鉢
も同じです。清浄心になるための手段であるわけです。

草庵茶がおこった室町中期以来、茶席のしつらえは、「市中の山居」を旨とするようにいわれてまいりました。
その「市中の山居」を演出する場が露地であったわけです。

利休居士が、ある茶人の朝会に招かれたときのことです。昨夜来の風に椋の木の葉が庭一面に散りつもって、
露地はさながら山中の林の道を歩くかのようでありました。居士はあとをふりかえりながら、「何とも風情のある
けしきではないか。しかし今日の亭主は茶の湯功者ではないから、この落ち葉を掃き捨ててしまうことでしょう」
といわれた。すると、はたして中立のときには、この落ち葉は一枚残らず掃除されておりました。

居士は露地の掃除とは、木の葉をきれいに取り去ってしまうだけではなく、表面に見える美ではない心の美を
大切にしなければならないということをいったものであります。

# A DISCLOSED SOUL OF "ROJI"   SEN SOSHITSU XV (Urasenke Grand Tea Master)

At the beginning of one of the "Nampo Roku", Sen Rikyu, the great master of "chanoyu", defines the Japanese traditional discipline of chanoyu as follows:

> There is shelter enough when the roof does not leak, and food, when it keeps one from starving. This is the Buddha's teaching and the fundamental intent of chanoyu. The practitioner brings water, gathers firewood, and boils the water. Making tea, he offers it to the Buddha, serves it to others, and drinks himself. He arranges flowers and burns incense. In all of this, he takes for model the acts of the Buddhas and patriarchs.   (Translation by Dennis Hirota, Chanoyu Quarterly, No. 25, 1980)

Rikyu, first of all, teaches "Chisoku anbun", i.e. "learn to be content" or "be content with a way of life in proportion to your means". One learns to be content, and only then does one make fire, bring water, boil it and prepare tea by one's own labor. The tea thus prepared is offered to the Buddha, then to people, and finally is partaken of oneself. This is the basic attitude in chanoyu. Here in lies the meaning of offering a bowl of tea.

In the "Nampo Roku", Rikyu also says that "wabi" (taste for the simple and quiet) expresses a Buddhist world of purity and cleanliness. He maintains that the chanoyu provides a place for practicing religion. The "roji" became necessary in order to establish chanoyu as a means for practicing one's belief.

In terms of chanoyu, the "roji" means the garden around a tea room. In a Buddhist interpretation, it means "arawa" or disclosure. It does not simply means "to disclose objects to the eyes" but "to disclose the body and soul", hence exposure of everything.

The host of a tea gathering cleans his "roji", the path where his guest passes, and waters it. He must first of all discard prejudices and evil passions, and cleanse himself.

The guest, too, must cleanse his hands and mouth at the "tsukubai", a stone basin in the garden, when he walks through the "roji". It is not, however, just a simple washing. The state of his mind at this moment must be such that "shinshin kore rojo" (both body and soul are clean and free from even one stain). After having washed his hands and mouth, the guest goes to the "nijiriguchi", the entrance to the tea room, where he takes off his shoes before entering the room. Some people might wonder if it is not a contradiction to handle one's shoes after having taken the trouble of washing one's hands. This question is raised out of ignorance to the very nature of the "roji". The "roji" is not a dirty place. It is a special space with everything around made neat and clean by the host himself with all his heart. He waters the path and trees alongside and swabs all the stepping stones.

One should regard it as another universe, clearly apart from this world. There is a Buddhist sutra which describes the "haku-roji" (open, exposed ground) as a place to live free from the three realms of existance, the past, present and future. If you think that you get dirty because you've touched your shoes after walking through the "roji", then there is no place you can go.

The act of washing one's hands and mouth at the "tsukubai" before going through the "nijiriguchi" is the same as that of purifying the body with holy water at a Christian church. The water of the "tsuku-bai" is considered sacred. The same thing holds true of the water basin at a Shinto shrine or a Buddhist temple as it is a means to make your body and soul pure.

Since the middle of the Muromachi Period (from the 14th to 16th century) when "soan cha", or chanoyu in a rustic hut emerged as one style of chanoyu, it has been believed that the whole installation for chanoyu must constitute "a mountain cottage in town". It is the "roji" which provides the setting for "a mountain cottage in town".

One day Rikyu was invited to a morning tea. Leaves of Muku (aphananthe aspera) trees had been blown off by wind blowing the night before and were lying thick all over the "roji", so that one felt as if one were walking along a path in a forest in the mountains. While looking back, Rikyu said "What a tasteful landscape! But, the host of today's tea is not a tactful master of chanoyu, so he will probably sweep away these leaves". In fact, when the participants came out of the tea room at the intermission during the tea, they found that all the fallen leaves had been swept away and not a single leaf was left.

Rikyu meant to say that cleaning the "roji" does not simply mean the action of removing fallen leaves; the concern should be the beauty not visible externally but manifest within one's heart.

*Design: Hiroto Kumagai*
デザイン：熊谷博人

*Editorial Director: Kakuzo Akahira*
エディトリアル・ディレクター：赤平覚三

1 銀閣寺 東求堂全景 室町時代 京都
*Ginkaku-ji Togu-do A Complete View*
*Muromachi Era Kyoto*

2 銀閣寺 東求堂内部より庭景観 室町時代 京都
*Ginkaku-ji A View from Togu-do Muromachi Era Kyoto*

3 銀閣寺 同仁斎全景 室町時代 京都
*Ginkaku-ji Doninsai A Complete View Muromachi Era Kyoto*

4 銀閣寺 同仁斎内部 室町時代 京都
*Ginkaku-ji The Inside of Doninsai Muromachi Era Kyoto*

5 大仙院 書院内部より庭景観 室町時代 京都
*Daisen-in A View from Study Room Muromachi Era Kyoto*

6 大仙院 書院内部より庭景観 室町時代 京都
*Daisen-in A View from Study Room Muromachi Era Kyoto*

7 桂離宮 松琴亭茶室前流れ手水石組 桃山時代 京都
*Katsura Rikyu Shokin-tei Tea Ceremony Room Washing Water Stone Grouping Momoyama Era Kyoto*

8 桂離宮 松琴亭茶室 桃山時代 京都
*Katsura Rikyu Shokin-tei Tea Ceremony Room Momoyama Era Kyoto*

9 桂離宮 腰掛待合 桃山時代 京都
*Katsura Rikyu Koshikake Waiting Bench Momoyama Era Kyoto*

10 桂離宮 腰掛待合砂雪隠 桃山時代 京都
*Katsura Rikyu Koshikake Waiting Bench*
*Suna-setchin Momoyama Era Kyoto*

11 表千家 不審庵中潜り 桃山時代 京都
*Omote Senke Fushin-an Nakakuguri*
*(Wicket Gate) Momoyama Era Kyoto*

12 表千家 不審庵梅見門と役石 桃山時代 京都
*Omote Senke Fushin-an Baiken-mon Gate and*
*Yakuishi Momoyama Era Kyoto*

13 表千家 不審庵腰掛待合全景 桃山時代 京都
*Omote Senke Fushin-an Koshikake Waiting*
*Bench A Complete View Momoyama Era Kyoto*

14 表千家 不審庵露地全景 桃山時代 京都
*Omote Senke Fushin-an Roji A Complete View Momoyama Era Kyoto*

15 如庵 全景 桃山時代 愛知
*Jo-an A Complete View Momoyama Era Aichi*

16 如庵 井筒付近 桃山時代 愛知
*Jo-an Around the Izutsu Momoyama Era Aichi*

17 裏千家 又隠全景 江戸時代 京都
*Urasenke Yuin A Complete View Edo Era Kyoto*

18 裏千家 又隠前蹲踞 江戸時代 京都
*Urasenke Yuin Tsukubai Edo Era Kyoto*

19 裏千家 猿戸付近 江戸時代 京都
*Urasenke Around the Sarudo Edo Era Kyoto*

20 裏千家 腰掛待合と役石 江戸時代 京都
*Urasenke Koshikake Waiting Bench and Yakuishi Edo Era Kyoto*

21 孤篷庵 忘筌露結手水鉢付近 江戸時代 京都
*Koho-an Bosen Around the Roketsu Water Basin Edo Era Kyoto*

22 孤篷庵 忘筌前軒内 江戸時代 京都
*Koho-an The Inside of Bosen Edo Era Kyoto*

23 孤篷庵 山雲床刀掛と刀掛石 江戸時代 京都
*Koho-an Sanunjo Sword Hanger and Hanger Stones Edo Era Kyoto*

24 修学院離宮 窮邃亭全景 江戸時代 京都
*Shugakuin Rikyu Kyutsui-tei A Complete View Edo Era Kyoto*

25 修学院離宮 窮邃亭内部 江戸時代 京都
*Shugakuin Rikyu The Inside of Kyutsui-tei Edo Era Kyoto*

26 修学院離宮 寿月観茶亭 江戸時代 京都
*Shugakuin Rikyu Jugetsukancha-tei*
*Edo Era Kyoto*

27 修学院離宮 寿月観前飛び石 江戸時代 京都
*Shugakuin Rikyu Jugetsukan Stepping Stones*
*Edo Era Kyoto*

28 藪内宗家燕庵 躙口付近 江戸時代 京都
*Yabunouchi Soke En-an Around*
*the Nijiriguchi Edo Era Kyoto*

29 藪内宗家燕庵 蹲踞文覚手水鉢 江戸時代 京都
*Yabunouchi Soke En-an Tsukubai Mongaku Water Basin Edo Era Kyoto*

30 藪内宗家 鉄砲垣と飛び石 江戸時代 京都
*Yabunouchi Soke Teppo-gaki and Stepping Stones Edo Era Kyoto*

31 仁和寺 飛涛亭貴人口と刀掛付近 江戸時代 京都
*Ninna-ji Hito-tei Around the Kijinguchi and Sword Hanger Edo Era Kyoto*

32 仁和寺 飛涛亭全景 江戸時代 京都
*Ninna-ji Hito-tei A Complete View Edo Era Kyoto*

33 仁和寺 飛涛亭内部 江戸時代 京都
*Ninna-ji The Inside of Hito-tei Edo Era Kyoto*

34 高台寺 傘亭全景 江戸時代 京都
*Kodai-ji Karakasa-tei A Complete View*
*Edo Era Kyoto*

35 高台寺 傘亭内部 江戸時代 京都
*Kodai-ji The Inside of Karakasa-tei*
*Edo Era Kyoto*

36 六窓庵 全景（東京国立博物館内）江戸時代 東京
*Rokuso-an A Complete View*
*(Tokyo National Museum) Edo Era Tokyo*

37 六窓庵 蹲踞付近 江戸時代 東京
*Rokuso-an Around the Tsukubai Edo Era Tokyo*

38 松花堂 茶堂全景 江戸時代 京都
*Shoka-do Tea Ceremony Room A Complete View Edo Era Kyoto*

39 松花堂 書院への曲り敷石 江戸時代 京都
*Shoka-do A Corner to Study Room Flagstones Edo Era Kyoto*

40 西翁院 中門付近 江戸時代 京都
*Saio-in Around the Middle Gate Edo Era Kyoto*

41 西翁院 澱看席躙口付近 江戸時代 京都
*Saio-in Yodomi-seki Around the Nijiriguchi Edo Era Kyoto*

42 西翁院 澱看席袈裟形蹲踞 江戸時代 京都
*Saio-in Yodomi-seki Kesa-gata Tsukubai Edo Era Kyoto*

43 高桐院 松向軒蹲踞付近 江戸時代 京都
*Koto-in Shoko-ken Around the Tsukubai*
*Edo Era Kyoto*

44 高桐院 松向軒躙口付近 江戸時代 京都
*Koto-in Shoko-ken Around the Nijiriguchi*
*Edo Era Kyoto*

45 居初氏天然図画亭 前庭 江戸時代 滋賀
*Mr. Izome's Tennenzuga-tei Front Garden Edo Era Shiga*

46 居初氏天然図画亭 立ち蹲踞 江戸時代 滋賀
*Mr. Izome's Tennenzuga-tei Tachi-tsukubai Edo Era Shiga*

47 西田氏玉泉園 書院前踏分石付近 江戸時代 石川
*Mr. Nishida's Gyokusen-en Around the Study Room Fumiwake Stepping Stones Edo Era Ishikawa*

48 西田氏玉泉園 東庭井戸付近 江戸時代 石川
*Mr. Nishida's Gyokusen-en Around the East Garden Well Edo Era Ishikawa*

49 西田氏玉泉園 寒雲亭前飛び石 江戸時代 石川
*Mr. Nishida's Gyokusen-en Kanun-tei Stepping Stones Edo Era Ishikawa*

50 西田氏玉泉園 本庭前踏分石と中門 江戸時代 石川
*Mr. Nishida's Gyokusen-en Main Garden Fumiwake Stepping Stones and*
*Middle Gate Edo Era Ishikawa*

51 西田氏玉泉園 灑雪亭と飛び石 江戸時代 石川
*Mr. Nishida's Gyokusen-en Saisetsu-tei and Stepping Stones Edo Era Ishikawa*

52 珠光庵 蹲踞(称名寺) 江戸時代 奈良
*Juko-an Tsukubai (Shomyo-ji) Edo Era Nara*

53 珠光庵 全景(称名寺) 江戸時代 奈良
*Juko-an A Complete View (Shomyo-ji) Edo Era Nara*

54 慈光院 書院遠望 江戸時代 奈良
*Jiko-in Study Room A Distant View Edo Era Nara*

55 慈光院 茶室内部 江戸時代 奈良
*Jiko-in The Inside of Tea Ceremony Room Edo Era Nara*

56 興聖寺 露地蹲踞 江戸時代 京都
*Kosho-ji Roji Tsukubai Edo Era Kyoto*

57 東陽坊 露地全景 江戸時代 京都
*Toyo-bo Roji A Complete View Edo Era Kyoto*

58 官休庵 腰掛待合 江戸時代 京都
*Kankyu-an Koshikake Waiting Bench*
*Edo Era Kyoto*

59 官休庵 躙口付近 江戸時代 京都
*Kankyu-an Around the Nijiriguchi*
*Edo Era Kyoto*

63 兼六園 夕顔亭全景 江戸時代 石川
*Kenroku-en Yugao-tei A Complete View*
*Edo Era Ishikawa*

64 兼六園 夕顔亭内部 江戸時代 石川
*Kenroku-en The Inside of Yugao-tei Edo Era Ishikawa*

65 兼六園 夕顔亭前邯鄲の手水鉢 江戸時代 石川
*Kenroku-en Yugao-tei Kantan Water Basin Edo Era Ishikawa*

66 桂春院 書院前飛び石と猿戸 江戸時代 京都
*Keishun-in Study Room Stepping Stones and Sarudo Edo Era Kyoto*

67 桂春院 方丈東庭飛び石と敷石 江戸時代 京都
*Keishun-in Hojo East Garden Stepping Stones and Flagstones Edo Era Kyoto*

68 浄土寺 露滴庵全景 江戸時代 広島
*Jodo-ji Roteki-an A Complete View Edo Era Hiroshima*

69 浄土寺 露滴庵待合 江戸時代 広島
*Jodo-ji Roteki-an Waiting Bench Edo Era Hiroshima*

70 古門堂 露地腰掛待合 江戸時代 島根
*Komon-do Roji Koshikake Waiting Bench Edo Era Shimane*

71 古門堂 躙口付近 江戸時代 島根
*Komon-do Around the Nijiriguchi Edo Era Shimane*

72 古門堂 露地敷石 江戸時代 島根
*Komon-do Roji Flagstones Edo Era Shimane*

73 古門堂 貴人口付近 江戸時代 島根
*Komon-do Around the Kijinguchi Edo Era Shimane*

74 古門堂 前滝石組 江戸時代 島根
*Komon-do Taki Stone Grouping Edo Era Shimane*

75 古門堂 滝前より茶室を望む 江戸時代 島根
*Komon-do Tea Ceremony Room Viewed from
the Waterfall Edo Era Shimane*

76 八窓庵 全景 江戸時代 奈良
*Hassou-an A Copmlete View Edo Era Nara*

77 玉林院 簑庵露地全景 江戸時代 京都
*Gyokurin-in Sa-an Roji A Copmlete View*
*Edo Era Kyoto*

78 三渓園 金毛窟全景 明治時代 神奈川
*Sankei-en Konmokutsu A Complete View Meiji Era Kanagawa*

79 三渓園 春草廬全景 明治時代 神奈川
*Sankei-en Shunsoro A Complete View Meiji Era Kanagawa*

80 芦花浅水荘 莎香亭前井戸付近 大正時代 滋賀
*Rokasensui-so Shako-tei Around the Well Taisho Era Shiga*

81 芦花浅水荘 記恩堂前蹲踞 大正時代 滋賀
*Rokasensui-so Kion-do Tsukubai Taisho Era Shiga*

82 小堀宗家 露地夜景 現代 東京
*Kobori Soke Roji A Night View Present Age Tokyo*

83 小堀宗家 躙口より蹲踞を見る 現代 東京
*Kobori Soke Tsukubai Viewed from the Nijiriguchi Present Age Tokyo*

84 大日本茶道学会 梅見門付近 現代 東京
*Tea Ceremony Association (Dainihon Chado
Gakkai) Around the Baiken-mon Gate
Present Age Tokyo*

85 大日本茶道学会 蹲踞 現代 東京
*Tea Ceremony Association (Dainihon Chado Gakkai) Tsukubai Present Age Tokyo*

86 松尾家露地 柴折戸付近 現代 愛知
*Mr. Matsuo's Roji Around the Shiorido Present Age Aichi*

87 松尾家露地 蹲踞 現代 愛知
*Mr. Matsuo's Roji Tsukubai Present Age Aichi*

88 吉田氏露地 梅見門付近 現代 愛知
*Mr. Yoshida's Roji Around the Baiken-mon*
*Gate Present Age Aichi*

89 吉田氏露地 蹲踞付近 現代 愛知
*Mr. Yoshida's Roji Around the Tsukubai Present Age Aichi*

90 小沢氏露地 全景 現代 宮城
*Mr. Ozawa's Roji A Complete View*
*Present Age Miyagi*

91 小沢氏蹲踞と光悦垣 現代 宮城
*Mr. Ozawa's Tsukubai and Koetsu-gaki Present Age Miyagi*

92 獨樂庵 露地全景 現代 東京
*Dokuraku-an Roji A Complete View Present Age Tokyo*

93 修禅寺 双皎山荘露地全景 現代 静岡
*Shuzen-ji Sokosanso Roji A Complete View Present Age Shizuoka*

94 岡崎氏露地 敷石と中門付近 現代 福岡
*Mr. Okazaki's Roji Around the Flagstones and*
*Middle Gate Present Age Fukuoka*

95 田中丸氏卍の腰掛待合 現代 福岡
*Mr. Tanakamaru's Fylfot Koshikake Waiting Room Present Age Fukuoka*

96 MOA 金の茶室全景 現代 静岡
*MOA's Golden Tea Ceremony Room A Complete View Present Age Shizuoka*

1　**銀閣寺** 東求堂全景 室町時代 京都

銀閣寺の正式な名称は慈照寺という。足利義政が祖父義満の金閣寺にならい造営した。東山を背景に写真の東求堂と観音殿（銀閣）は西芳寺の庭を参考にして造られたという。池庭の中に浮んでいる様は、美しい。

LINHOF KARDAN SYMMAR 180mm F16 1/15 EPR

2　**銀閣寺** 東求堂内部より庭景観 室町時代 京都

この部屋（仏間）の右側に義政公の御像が安置されている。正面に見える青石の石橋は仙袖橋と呼ばれ、池庭全体のなかでも古い部分といわれている。この仏間の奥に同仁斎があり、書院茶席初期の遺構とされ、つとに有名なものである。

LINHOF KARDAN FUJINON 120mm F22 1/4 EPR

3　**銀閣寺** 同仁斎全景 室町時代 京都

四畳半書院同仁斎の外観である。東求堂は祖先の位牌を祀る持仏堂として義政が特に力を入れて築造したと伝えられている。本尊を阿弥陀仏と定め、周囲の池に蓮が植えられていたという。浄土の荘厳を再現希求したのであろう。

LINHOF KARDAN NIKKOR 90mm F11 1/15 EPR

4　**銀閣寺** 同仁斎内部 室町時代 京都

同仁斎が初期茶室か否かは判然としないが、東求堂が造られた東山時代が茶の湯の基礎が確立した時代であることを考えあわせると、始めから茶を喫するための茶室ではなく、義政が書斎として活用しながら茶を喫したことは考えられる。

LINHOF KARDAN SUPERANGULON 75mm F11 ストロボ使用

5　**大仙院** 書院内部より庭景観 室町時代 京都

枯山水で有名な大仙院書院生苔室である通常は板戸で閉めてあり、右側が床になっていて書院風な構えになっている。かつてこの部屋で秀吉と利休が茶を喫し廊下前にある沈香石に花を生け秀吉が賞讃したという故事がある。

SINAR P NIKKOR 90mm F8 1/15 EPR

6　**大仙院** 書院内部より庭景観 室町時代 京都

礼の間からの眺めである。このように板戸や障子を取り払うという、いわば芝居の書割のような構成は秀吉の茶室を組立て式にして持ち運んだというユニークな発想に似て面白い。仏家の融通無碍の世界が見えて楽しい。

SINAR P SUPERANGULON 75mm F16 1/15 EPR

7　**桂離宮** 松琴亭茶室前流れ手水石組 桃山時代 京都

桂離宮には四つの茶屋がある。今のような茶湯専用の茶室ではない。食事をし、休息し、お茶を飲むという設備をもつ建物である。写真に示す流れの手水は多くある手水石組でも代表的なもの。庭の水、流れを蹲踞に見立てている。

SINAR P NIKKOR 90mm F11 1/60 EPR

8　**桂離宮** 松琴亭茶室 桃山時代 京都

松琴亭へ行く道すがらである。飛び石は少し高く勾配をもちながら白川橋へと誘導する。右下に前頁の流れ手水石組が見える。最近奇麗に修復整備され一段と美しくなったこのあたり水面に映えて際立っている。

SINAR P SUPERANGULON 75mm F11 1/15 EPR

9　**桂離宮** 腰掛待合 桃山時代 京都

松琴亭の腰掛待合である。この腰掛に坐って正面を見ると巨大な蘇鉄が林立している。この時代の庭園にはこの蘇鉄の植込みが多く目につく。右から左への延段敷石の左端に有名な二重枡形の手水鉢があり全体を引締めている。

SINAR P SUPERANGULON 75mm F11 1/15 EPR

10　**桂離宮** 腰掛待合砂雪隠 桃山時代 京都

茶庭には砂雪隠と下腹雪隠が必ず備えてある。雪隠とは便所のことであるが、砂雪隠は客が内部を拝見するのが礼の一つになっている。内部は足を乗せる石組と白砂で構成され、独特な形をもっている。下腹雪隠はほんとの便所。

SINAR P SUPERANGULON 75mm F16 1秒 EPR

11　**表千家** 不審庵中潜り 桃山時代 京都

茶庭には外露地と内露地の区別があり、その間に中潜りがある。中門の役目をもつ。利休時代にはないとされているが私はあったのではないかと思っている。茶室の躙口のように蹲って出入する形をもっているのも共通性がある。

LINHOF KARDAN SUPERANGULON 75mm F16 1/2 EPR

12　**表千家** 不審庵梅見門と役石 桃山時代 京都

不審庵への役石と中門である。茶庭の中で客と亭主が始めて挨拶を交す場所でもある。この中門を潜ると右に腰掛待合、飛び石づたい左に不審庵がある。このあたりの侘びた風情は一種の緊迫感が漲りぴりりとする。

LINHOF KARDAN SUPERANGULON 75mm F16 1秒 EPR

**13 表千家 不審庵腰掛待合全景 桃山時代 京都**

客はこの腰掛待合に坐し、茶室に入るのを待つ。入室への合図があるまでの時間は期待感が強く漂う。どんな茶事が待っているのかと心ふくらみ、はずむ瞬間でもある。飛び石の打ち水が美しく、溢れる清浄感はあたりを仏う。

LINHOF KARDAN NIKKOR 90mm F22 1/4 EPR

**14 表千家 不審庵露地全景 桃山時代 京都**

露地茶庭は茶室を中心とした空間である。そこには山あり川あり谷あり野道ありで、日本の風景が凝縮されている。深く植え込まれた樹々は森、飛び石、敷石は獣道かもしれない。ゆるい勾配のあるのは坂道だ。それが茶庭では。

LINHOF KARDAN NIKKOR 90mm F22 1/2 EPR

**15 如庵 全景 桃山時代 愛知**

織田有楽は信長の弟。信長の死後秀吉に従い、後出家し如庵有楽と号した。この茶室は再三の移転をくり返し、現在の犬山市に落ち着いた。別名暦の席ともいう。貴人口と躙口が特色で、草庵と書院風が同居している。

SINAR P NIKKOR 90mm F11 1/30 EPR

**16 如庵 井筒付近 桃山時代 愛知**

茶事に良い水は欠かせない。茶庭には必ず井戸井筒がある。石材を井桁に組んだり、円形、方形にくり抜き組み上げられたものがある。この井筒は「佐女牛井」の名があり元和元年九月二日有楽の銘が陰刻されている。

SINAR P SYMMAR 150mm F22 1/2 EPR

**17 裏千家 又隠全景 江戸時代 京都**

また隠れるの意味をもつ裏千家を代表する茶庭である。千宗旦は利休の孫、江岑宗左に不審庵を譲り仙叟宗室に今日庵を任せ自分はこの又隠を経営した。躙口前の通称豆撒石の飛び石は宗旦自ら無作意に配したという。

SINAR P NIKKOR 90mm F22 1秒 EPR

**18 裏千家 又隠前蹲踞 江戸時代 京都**

利休遺愛の手水鉢である。鎌倉時代の層塔の塔身を利用したもので、四方に仏の姿が彫ってあり美しい形をしている。周囲に多くの植栽を配し、あくまでも深く隠された侘びの表現は心憎い演出で奥ゆかしい。

SINAR P NIKKOR 90mm F22 1秒 EPR

**19 裏千家 猿戸付近 江戸時代 京都**

今にも亭主と客がそこにいて挨拶を交しているような雰囲気をもつこのあたり野筋の感が強い。昔から猿戸は利休が作り、中潜りは織部が創作し、中門は遠州が考えたといわれている。打ち水された役石が美しい。

SINAR P NIKKOR 90mm F22 1秒 EPR

**20 裏千家 腰掛待合と役石 江戸時代 京都**

無色軒前にある腰掛待合である。腰掛左隅に立派な貴人石を一つ据え、客石は大籔の延段風になっている。付近の役石はさすがにいいなあという気品と格式をもっている。右下露地帯のあたりの塵穴も形がいい。

SINAR P SUPERANGULON 75mm F22 5秒 レフ使用

**21 孤蓬庵 忘筌露結手水鉢付近 江戸時代 京都**

一休和尚を始め村田珠光、利休等人徳寺と茶湯の関係はひときわ深い。中でも遠州の菩提寺孤蓬庵忘筌の席は他に類を見ない構成を見せている。四枚腰無障子を引き違いにして景色が変るという発想は並のものではない。

LINHOF KARDAN SUPERANGULON 90mm F22 1/4 EPR

**22 孤蓬庵 忘筌前軒内 江戸時代 京都**

孤蓬庵は小堀遠州により竜光院内に創立された。寛永二十年現地に移転火災で焼失したが、近衛家や松平不昧等の援助で再建された。軒内の飛び石は火災のためいたんでいるが、遠州時代そのままだといわれている。

LINHOF KARDAN FUJINON 120mm F22 1/8 EPR

**23 孤蓬庵 山雲床刀掛と刀掛石 江戸時代 京都**

茶室の中は貴人も武家も町人も上下の隔はないという主張から、武士の帯刀は許されない。そこで考案されたこの山雲床の刀掛石は何百年か前の樹の化石が据えられている。またその切り口が樹を切ったようになっているのも素晴しい。

LINHOF KARDAN NIKKOR 90mm F22 1/2 EPR

**24 修学院離宮 窮邃亭全景 江戸時代 京都**

修学院離宮の御茶屋は上、中、下三つの御茶屋に区別される。窮邃亭は上の御茶屋にあり眺望の一番きく中島にある下部の浴竜池を通しての京都北方、西山の景観は日本庭園中第一級のものであろう。紅葉の頃また美しい。

SINAR P NIKKOR 90mm F16 1/60 EPR

**25 修学院離宮 窮邃亭内部 江戸時代 京都**

修学院は御水尾院のため徳川氏が経営した。室内は眺望本位の間取りで、西、北に大きく高く軒を取っていて、写真に見る中央一段高くなっている所が上皇の御座になっている。上部にある御額は上皇御自身の御宸筆である。

SINAR P SUPERANGULON 75mm F11 1秒 EPR

**26 修学院離宮 寿月観茶亭 江戸時代 京都**

寿月観の御茶屋は下の茶屋にあり、後水尾院の御座所だった。文政年間再建されたが、創建当時のまま復旧された。すぐ前に遣水があり、滝口から微かな水音が聞こえ別世界を現出している。寿月観の御額も御宸筆である。

LINHOF KARDAN NIKKOR 90mm F22 1/2 EPR

**27 修学院離宮 寿月観前飛び石 江戸時代 京都**

御廊下上からの飛び石景観である。中央に形のいい踏分石があり、大きく右に振り三の間へと続く。まっすぐに進むと遣水の沢渡石に続き、苑路づたいに三角形の石を富士の山に見立てた白糸の滝と呼ばれる滝口に続く。

LINHOF KARDAN NIKKOR 90mm F22 1/15 EPR

**28 薮内宗家燕庵 躙口付近 江戸時代 京都**

薮内家は西本願寺の茶道師家で、武家風な書院点前を基本としている。初代剣仲は古田織部の妹を娶っているので、義兄弟ということになる。露地のありさまは貴人に対する配慮が随所に見られ、その典型は腰掛待合に代表される。

LINHOF KARDAN NIKKOR 90mm F22 1/2 EPR

**29 薮内宗家燕庵 蹲踞文覚手水鉢 江戸時代 京都**

鎌倉期の五輪塔の水輪を利用した手水鉢である。この五輪塔が文覚上人の居住地にあったことからこの名がある。手水鉢には石造物を利用した物が多い。礎石、灯篭、橋杭、宝塔、宝篋印塔、無縫塔、層塔等見立て物として使われている。

LINHOF KARDAN NIKKOR 150mm F22 1/2 EPR

**30 薮内宗家 鉄砲垣と飛び石 江戸時代 京都**

燕庵を出て露地口に向かう飛び石が美しい。はるか向うに西の屋形灯篭も見え、鉄砲垣沿いの道すがらは草庵風というより貴人がお小姓を連れ大股に濶歩して行くといった雰囲気が漂っている――というと私の思い込みだろうか。

LINHOF KARDAN NIKKOR 90mm F22 1/4 EPR

**31 仁和寺 飛涛亭貴人口と刀掛付近 江戸時代 京都**

御室の仁和寺は門跡寺院である。池泉を通して見える飛涛亭は光格天皇遺愛の席といわれ貴人席である。右側に刀掛石と刀掛があるがこの刀掛石も化石を使っている。草庵風な茶室と違っておおらかでゆったりしているのが心地よい。

LINHOF KARDAN SUPERANGULON 75mm F16 1/25 EPR

**32 仁和寺 飛涛亭全景 江戸時代 京都**

ここ仁和寺には有名な茶亭が二つある。飛涛亭と遼廓亭である。遼廓亭前の草庵風な流れや石橋を横に見て深い木立を進むと、渓流をへだてて美しい貴人口が飛び石とともに樹間に見えてくるさまは山家にたどり着いた感じになる。

LINHOF KARDAN SYMMAR 150mm F22 1/2 EPR

**33 仁和寺 飛涛亭内部 江戸時代 京都**

右側の円窓を飛涛の大海に太陽が昇った構成だという。そういわれればそんな気にもなる演出力をもっている。床の間を全面土で塗り込んである床を洞床という。昭和十二年国宝に、同二十五年重要文化財に指定されている。

LINHOF KARDAN NIKKOR 75mm F11 ストロボ使用 EPR

**34 高台寺 傘亭全景 江戸時代 京都**

京都高台寺の境内にある傘亭は伏見城より移築されたと伝えられている。利休好みといわれているが確証はない。隣の時雨亭と吹き抜けの廊下でつながっている形は茶亭のなかでも変っていて有名なものである。

SINAR P SYMMAR 150mm F22 1/30 EPR

**35 高台寺 傘亭内部 江戸時代 京都**

吹き抜けの廊下でつながっている時雨亭という名前と対象的に傘亭と名付けて傘のパターンを作り上げた発想は誰のものなのか。化粧屋根裏の造型がまた面白い放射状に傘を広げた形になっているさまはユニークだ。

LINHOF KARDAN SUPERANGULON 75mm F8 ストロボ使用 EPR

**36 六窓庵 全景(東京国立博物館内) 江戸時代 東京**

もと奈良興福寺慈眼院にあったものを東京帝室博物館が購入し館の苑内に復元した。慶安年中、金森宗和の好みで建てられたという。こんな形で茶室は移転をくり返しながら生きてきた例は実に多い。

SINAR P FIJINON 120mm F11 1/15 EPR

**37 六窓庵 蹲踞付近 江戸時代 東京**

茶庭の蹲踞もずいぶん見てきたが、たいていの場合このようにして竹樋で水を落している。特に関東方面に多い。茶事に用いるとき、水は亭主が運び入れ清潔にし客を待つ。この場合の蹲踞は多分に茶庭の景として取り扱っているのであろう。

LINHOF KARDAN NIKKOR 180mm F22 1/2 EPR

**38 松花堂 茶堂全景 江戸時代 京都**

松花堂昭乗の茶堂である。茅葺宝形造りの小堂で、内部は二畳、仏壇、置水屋、袋棚、竈戸が作られ、小さな住居の形をした草庵である。天井に日輪と鳳凰を極彩色で描かれているさまは素朴な外観とは裏腹に息をのむ。

LINHOF KARDAN SUPERANGULON 75mm F16 1/4 EPR

**39 松花堂 書院への曲り敷石 江戸時代 京都**

松花堂露地はもと石清水八幡宮にあったものを、明治二十四年現地に泉坊の庭とともに移築復元された。泉坊前の庭は、相当改造されているがこの茶堂付近は全体として当初の姿が守られているようで美しい。

LINHOF KARDAN FUJINON 120mm F22 1/2 EPR

**40 西翁院 中門付近 江戸時代 京都**

西翁院は黒谷金戒光明寺の塔頭で、滋賀の居初氏天然図画亭の茶庭とともに藤村庸軒を代表する遺構として有名である。写真に示す外露地の中門あたり清楚な感じが心地よい。

SINAR P SYMMAR 150mm F22 1/15 EPR

**41 西翁院 澱看席躙口付近 江戸時代 京都**

藤村庸軒は千宗旦の門弟で、四天王の一人といわれたくらい千家の奥義を極めた。この西翁院の西北高台に庸軒の営んだ反古庵と呼ぶ窓から淀川、山崎が遠望できたことから席名を澱(淀)看席といわれるようになったという。

SINAR P NIKKOR 90mm F22 1/15 EPR

**42 西翁院 澱看席袈裟形蹲踞 江戸時代 京都**

澱看席躙口前にある袈裟形の手水鉢である。普通蹲踞というと灯篭などを含めた形なのだが、ここではそれがない。庸軒手植の檜の大木の下、でんと据えられている。右に湯桶石、左に手燭石、前石役石が揃った形は美しい。

SINAR P NIKKOR 150mm F22 1/5 EPR

**43 高桐院 松向軒蹲踞付近 江戸時代 京都**

松向軒前の蹲踞である。小振りながら織部灯篭を従へた形は、ひなびた中にもりんとした存在感がある。前石を前面に大きく取った手法も巧者の仕事であろう。適当な繁りも草庵露地の雰囲気をよく伝えている。

LINHOF KARDAN FUJINON 120mm F22 2秒 EPR

**44 高桐院 松向軒躙口付近 江戸時代 京都**

高桐院は細川三斎が父幽斎の菩提を弔うため創建した。境内に利休から譲り受けた灯篭が三斎の墓標として祀られている。席名は北野大茶会の折北野経堂前の影向の松付近に設けた茶室に因むもので、室内に「松向」の扁額がかかっている。

LINHOF KARDAN SUPERANGULON 75mm F22 2秒 EPR

**45 居初氏天然図画亭 前庭 江戸時代 滋賀**

堅田浮御堂のあたり旧街道沿いに居初家はある。堅田水軍の総帥で、代々庄家を務めた旧家である。庭園は書院庭と露地庭がうまくからみあい、解りやすい庭になっている。天気のよい日には近江富士が遠望でき借景となる。

SINAR P FUJINON 120mm F22 1/60 EPR

**46 居初氏天然図画亭 立ち蹲踞 江戸時代 滋賀**

形のいいこの立蹲踞あたり、直線の大畿の敷石が目を引く。書院露地風の典雅な構成は藤村庸軒と北村幽安の合作という。右に湯桶石、左に手燭石、前石と典型的な立ち蹲踞の姿はきりりとして一寸の隙もない。

SINAR P SYMMAR 150mm F22 1/30 EPR

**47 西田氏玉泉園 書院前踏分石付近 江戸時代 石川**

書院(西庭)前の飛び石である。大振りに打たれた飛び石は雪国には珍しく高く打っていない。中央の大きな石が踏分石、優しく右に振っている。その左側に芭を彫り出した飾り蹲踞がある。石造としては立派なもので堂々としている。

SINAR P NIKKOR 90mm F22 1/2 EPR

**48 西田氏玉泉園 東庭井戸付近 江戸時代 石川**

加賀百万石の城下町大名庭園で有名な兼六園のすぐそばに玉泉園はある。兼六園の樹林が借景の東庭である。この脇の飛び石を伝って行くと瀧雪亭に出る。荒々しい井桁の組み方は力強く逞しい。

SINAR P FUJINON 120mm F22 1秒 EPR

49 **西田氏玉泉園** 寒雲亭前飛び石 江戸時代 石川

寒雪亭前飛び石である。寒雲亭は裏千家にある茶室の一つで、宗旦好みと伝えられる。書院茶席で西田家の寒雲亭は写しである。だからこの飛び石も草庵風ではなく、何かしらおおらかさがあり気品がある。

SINAR P SIMMAR 150mm F22 1/2 EPR

50 **西田氏玉泉園** 本庭前踏分石と中門 江戸時代 石川

玉泉園このあたり右側に池泉庭園があり微かに山畔上部から滝音が聞こえてくる。江戸初期廻遊式庭園である。この飛び石づたいに中門を潜ると山上の瀧雪亭に出る。このあたりから草庵風な色合いが濃くなってくる。

SINAR P FUJINON 120mm F22 1/2 EPR

51 **西田氏玉泉園** 瀧雪亭と飛び石 江戸時代 石川

初代脇田直賢から四代にわたってこの庭は完成される。二代直能は仙叟宗室に師事した関係から、瀧雪亭露地を指導したという。雪の深い所から軒内を広く取り飛び石も高く打っている雪国らしい構図だ。

SINAR P FUJINON 90mm F22 1/2 EPR

52 **珠光庵** 蹲踞(称名寺) 江戸時代 奈良

奈良称名寺にある茶席は村田珠光ゆかりと伝える。珠光は足利義政に仕え一休禅師に参禅、茶禅一体の草庵茶を始めたといわれている。蹲踞は水穴がひときわ大きくくってあり実用を重視したものと思われる。

SINAR P FUJINON 120mm F16 1/30 EPR

53 **珠光庵** 全景(称名寺) 江戸時代 奈良

正面に大きく貴人口が設けられている。しかし沓脱石も小さく濡れ縁をつけ気負ったところがない。刀掛石も小さく刀掛も控え目である。これが茶祖珠光の心根か、と思うのは私だけだろうか。

SINAR P SUPERANGULON 75mm F16 1/2 EPR

54 **慈光院** 書院遠望 江戸時代 奈良

入母屋造茅葺屋根は書院屋根というより田舎家風である。近くに流れる冨雄川畔からの遠望である。この中に石州流の祖片桐石見守貞昌が好んだ茶室がある。開放的でおおらかな武家の心がくみとれる。

MAMIYA R2 SEKOR 150mm F16 1/30 EPR

55 **慈光院** 茶室内部 江戸時代 奈良

書院上の間から見た景観は素晴らしい。奈良の山々を大きく取り込んだ借景は、庭の大刈込に溶けこんでパノラマ風に展開する。写真は石州が好んだといわれる二畳台目に床をつけ二畳の控えの間をつけた席である。

LINHOF KARDAN SUPERANGULON 75mm ストロボ使用 EPR

56 **興聖寺** 露地蹲踞 江戸時代 京都

興聖寺には古田織部の墓がある。織部は利休の高弟であるが師の利休とは正反対といっていい。織部流では薄茶でも茶碗が台子に乗っているという具合である。織部灯篭を奥に重厚な伽藍石がいかにも大名の蹲踞らしい。

SINAR P FUJINON 120mm F22 1秒 EPR

57 **東陽坊** 露地全景 江戸時代 京都

大本山建仁寺本坊にある名席。東陽坊とは利休門下の茶人で真如堂山内東陽坊の住職であった。北野大茶会の折紙屋川の土手にこの茶室を作ったものといわれるが定かではない。

SINAR P NIKKOR 90mm F22 F1/10 EPR

58 **官休庵** 腰掛待合 江戸時代 京都

官休庵の庵名には二つの解釈がある。初代一翁が官を辞するとき官を休むという意味と、普通の自分を離れて茶道に没頭するという意味が込められているという。何か思いつめた意志が強く感じられる庵名ではないか。

SINAR P NIKKOR 90mm F22 1/2 EPR

59 **官休庵** 躙口付近 江戸時代 京都

武者小路千家の初代一翁宗守は千宗旦の次男として生まれた。高松藩への仕官を辞したとき寛文七年にこの茶室を造立したものと伝えている。躙口踏石東側の袖垣が侘草庵風な趣きを強めていて飛び石の向う編笠門が夕日に映えて美しい。

SINAR P SUPERANGULON 75mm F22 3秒 EPR

60 **官休庵** 環翠園前伽藍石手水鉢 江戸時代 京都

環翠園は武者小路千家の書院茶席である。その前に据えられている手水鉢で伽藍石形、美しい形をしている。ただ湯桶石、手燭石の役石が非常に低く据えられているのが特徴となっている。

LINHOF KARDAN FUJINON 120mm 1/2 EPR

61 **官休庵** 中門前飛び石と待合 江戸時代 京都

編笠門(中門)前の飛び石である。中央真ん中にあるのか踏分石。中門の下には伽藍石の乗越石が見える。中門を越えると茶室のほうへ、そのまま飛び石づたいに直進すると待合といった構図である。打ち水を施した景色は別世界にいるよう。

SINAR P NIKKOR 90mm F22 1秒 EPR

62 **官休庵** 留石 江戸時代 京都

留石である。別の名関守石ともいう露地の飛び石の分れ道なぞに置いて客の通行を制限する役目をもつ。留石から向うへは行けませんよという暗黙の信号なのである。露地の景として置いてあることもある。

SINAR P NIKKOR 210mm F22 1/2 EPR

63 **兼六園** 夕顔亭全景 江戸時代 石川

兼六園は日本三大名園の一つ。その園内瓢池の前に武家風な薮内燕庵形式の茶室がある。夕顔亭という。すぐ前に大瀑布があるので滝見亭とも呼ばれている。軒内土間庇が雪国らしく深い。宝形造りの形が美しい。

SINAR P NIKKOR 90mm F22 1/15 EPR

64 **兼六園** 夕顔亭内部 江戸時代 石川

三方に設けられた上がり口は、南側に躙口、西側に貴人口、北側は相伴席に通じている。朱の塗壁は美しく夕方など西日を受けた室内からの景は素晴らしく高貴な人の茶室という思いを強くする。

SINAR P SUPERANGULON 75mm F16 ストロボ使用

65 **兼六園** 夕顔亭前邯鄲の手水鉢 江戸時代 石川

奥深い土間庇が三方に廻らされた縁先に円形の手水鉢がある。邯鄲の手水鉢という水穴上面に邯鄲の夢の枕の故事を陽刻してあるのでこの名がある。後藤程乗という江戸初期に生きた金工師の作。

SINAR P FUJINON 120mm F22 1/2 EPR

66 **桂春院** 書院前飛び石と猿戸 江戸時代 京都

妙心寺山内桂春院には既白庵と呼ぶ茶室と茶庭がある。藤村庸軒との関係が深く現在もここの住職は茶道庸軒流の家元として指導に当っている。露地は上、下二段に分れていて写真に示すのは上部既白庵の露地である。

SINAR P NIKKON 90mm F22 1/25 EPR

67 桂春院 方丈東庭飛び石と敷石 江戸時代 京都

下部方丈東庭の飛び石、敷石の部分である。手前飛び
石と延段は方丈へとつながっている。このあたり植栽
多く山道の道すがらの趣きがあるが、一般の庭園と露
地風が混合していて区別がつきにくい。

SINAR P FUJINON 120mm F22 1/15 EPR

68 浄土寺 露滴庵全景 江戸時代 広島

広島尾道の浄土寺は聖徳太子開基の伝承のある古刹。
豊臣秀吉が愛用した茶室で、伏見城から移築された。
燕庵形式で織部好みの特色がよく踏襲しているという。
品性のよい飛び石が気持よく打たれていて華やかさも
感じられる。

SINAR P NIKKOR 90mm F22 1/15 EPR

69 浄土寺 露滴庵待合 江戸時代 広島

非常に個性の強い待合である。貴人席待合で明るい華
やいだ感じが満ちている。左側貴人石を一段高く据え、
客石は切り石である。客席上の格子は引き違いになっ
ていて、右、左に引くと外光が消えるようになっている。

SINAR P NIKKOR 90mm F22 1/30 EPR

70 古門堂 露地腰掛待合 江戸時代 島根

島根県安来市清水寺山内蓮乗院にある露地茶室である。
文化年中本寺の住職得故庵慧教和尚が建造した。慧教
和尚は細川三斎流を修得していた。一山修理の際、清
水寺の大門の古材を得て造ったのがこの茶室である。
ゆえにこの席を古門堂と称するようになったという。
この写真は、貴人席風な待合である左側に貴人席、客
席には円座（座布団）煙草盆がしつらえられていて、
客待ちの構へがしてある。

MAMIYA R2 SEKOR 50~105mm F11~22 シャッター1/30~1/2

71 古門堂 躙口付近 江戸時代 島根

躙口であるひときわ高い踏石が印象的だ。刀掛石もこ
じんまりしていて文人風なにおいがする。

MAMIYA R2 SEKOR 50~105mm F11~22 シャッター1/30~1/2

72 古門堂 露地敷石 江戸時代 島根

露地敷石に古瓦を利用している。立ち蹲踞には手水鉢
を置き、飾り鉢前の景である。

MAMIYA R2 SEKOR 50~105mm F11~22 シャッター1/30~1/2

73 古門堂 貴人口付近 江戸時代 島根

貴人口である。格式ばらない風情が好ましい。四つ目
垣を隔てての景はやはり文人調である。

MAMIYA R2 SEKOR 50~105mm F11~22 シャッター1/30~1/2

74 古門堂 前滝石組 江戸時代 島根

古門堂には雄竜、雌滝がある。雄滝前飛び石の景色で
ある。優しい雰囲気をかもし出している。

MAMIYA R2 SEKOR 50~105mm F11~22 シャッター1/30~1/2

75 古門堂 滝前より茶室を望む 江戸時代 島根

正面四つ目垣の向うが茶室である。ここらあたりは露
地風な繁みをみせている。

MAMIYA R2 SEKOR 50~105mm F11~22 シャッター1/30~1/2

76 八窓庵 全景 江戸時代 奈良

興福寺の寺坊大乗院の庭内にあったものを明治二十五
年現地に移築した。かつては含翠亭と呼んでいた。古
田織部好みといわれている前面横一列の飛び石中央の
やや大きい踏分石から軒内躙口へと向かう刀掛石は小
振りで優しい。

SINOR P NIKKOR 180mm F22 1/30 EPR

77 玉林院 簑庵露地全景 江戸時代 京都

大徳寺塔頭玉林院にある茶室である。大阪の富豪 鴻池
了英が建てた位牌堂南明庵に附属する。表千家七代如
心斎の指導を得て完成された。大霰敷きの延段にむく
れた地苔がからみつき踏み歩くのも悪いくらい美しい。

LINHOF KARDAN NIKKOR 90mm F22 1/15 EPR

78 三渓園 金毛窟全景 明治時代 神奈川

原三渓は名を冨太郎号を三渓といった。岐阜の豪農の
家に生まれ事業に大成功した後、古美術への憧憬が深
く横浜本牧に大庭園を造った。金毛窟は三渓翁が愛し
た茶室で、大徳寺山門の高欄の架木を用いているので
この名がある。

LINHOF KARDAN NIKKOR 90mm F22 1/2 EPR

79 三渓園 春草廬全景 明治時代 神奈川

もと宇治三室戸金蔵院にあった茶室で、大正七年三渓
園に移築された。窓の数が多く九窓あるところから九
窓亭ともいわれる。写真の露地右側に見事な伽藍石、
左側に蹲踞があり、自然石をくり抜いた素朴な手水鉢
は奥ゆかしい。

LINHOF KARDAN NIKKOR 90mm F22 1/2 EPR

80 芦花浅水荘 莎香亭前井戸付近 大正時代 滋賀

京都日本画壇の雄山元春挙画伯の自邸である。自分で
設計監督し、この庭を作った。私はこの芒の植栽が大
好きなのだ。いつお邪魔しても同じような繁り具合、
背の高さも変りないその手入れに、茶の心がみえて嬉
しい。

LINHOF KARDAN NIKKOR 28mm F22 1/30 EPR

81 芦花浅水荘 記恩堂前蹲踞 大正時代 滋賀

形のいい四方仏の手水鉢が中鉢形式に据えてある。中
鉢形式とは周囲をかこむようにふち取って中央に据え
ることをいう。松尾流家元の蹲踞にもそれがある。石
造美術品をよく見せるための構図である。

LINHOF KARDAN FUJINON 180mm F22 1/15 EPR

82 小堀宗家 露地夜景 現代 東京

東京信濃町の遠州流宗家家元の成趣庵露地である。細
長い地割りに白川砂と築山、地苔が素晴らしく美しい。
庭中央に流れがある。枝折戸四ツ目垣が低く設けてあ
り、結界となっている、その夜景である。この世とは
思えない幽玄な世界が現出している。

LINHOF KARDAN NIKKOR 90mm F11 8秒~20秒 EPR

83 小堀宗家 躙口より蹲踞を見る 現代 東京

江戸初期の大名であり茶人でもある小堀遠州の直系十
二代家元の茶庭蹲踞である。自然石の手水鉢が草庵風
な雰囲気をかもしだしている。前石と飛び石の濃淡が
調和してきれいさびが効いている。

LINHOF KARDAN NIKKOR 90mm F22 1/2 EPR

84 大日本茶道学会 梅見門付近 現代 東京

大日本茶道学会の創始者田中仙樵は茶道に流儀は必要
なしという理念で茶道会に新風を吹きこんだ茶匠。京
都に出て前田瑞雪宅に寄宿し修行。今日庵より奥儀を
受伝した。写真は槐南軒の東側縁より見た中門である。

SINAR P NIKKOR 90mm F22 1/2 EPR

85 大日本茶道学会 蹲踞 現代 東京

茶室知水亭前の蹲踞である宝塔の塔身を利用した手水
鉢は周囲の役石とともにてらいがなく渋い風情がある。
背後にある六角灯篭は北野天満宮の灯篭にそっくりで
深い植栽とともに侘びの世界を現出している。

SINNAR P FUJINON 120mm F22 1秒 EPR

**86 松尾家露地 柴折戸付近 現代 愛知**

茶道松尾流家元の茶庭である。十代不染斎好みて昭和
二十八年茶庭と茶室が完成された。主屋座敷から細長
い露地を隔てて松隠亭がある。枝折戸付近の役石は定
法どおり打たれ草庵風な雰囲気が濃い風情となってい
る。
LINHOF KARDAN NIKKOR 90mm F22 1/10 EPR

**87 松尾家露地 蹲踞 現代 愛知**

松尾流松隠亭の蹲踞である。席内部より撮影したもの
で、筒形の手水鉢は格好のいい作りである。海の部分
を多く取り、その雄大な構へとともに前石は大ぶりな
石をでんと据えている。湯桶石を低く手燭台を高く据
えているのは理にかなっている。
LINHOF KARDAN NIKKOR 90mm F22 1/2 EPR

**88 吉田氏露地 梅見門付近 現代 愛知**

吉田家は名古屋において代々表千家流を継承してきた。
昭和二十四年即中斎宗左から皆伝を許された表千家を
代表する茶家である。この梅見門あたり目だたない飛
び石の打ち方は控え目で優しい。門の手前左に腰掛待
合がある。
SINAR P NIKKOR 90mm F22 1/5 EPR

**89 吉田氏露地 蹲踞付近 現代 愛知**

この露地は先代紹村か昭和二十四、五年頃完成させた。
四方仏の蹲踞は安閑亭のもので、二方勝手の構えで作
られている。向う側から使えるし、こちら広間前から
も使えるという形である。だから役石も相対している。
SINAR P FUJINON 120mm F22 1/2 EPR

**90 小沢氏露地 全景 現代 宮城**

小沢邸は東北の旧家で現在医院を経営されている。玄
関の門が素晴らしい。その奥、主屋の左手にこの茶室
がある。秋の一日訪れたが、銀杏の木が夕日に映えて
黄金色に輝いていた。重森三玲の高弟小山雅久設計。
SINAR P NIKKOR 90mm F11 1/60 EPR

**91 小沢氏蹲踞と光悦垣 現代 宮城**

前頁の小山雅久氏の設計である。銭形の手水鉢と品格
のある埋め込み灯篭が美しい光悦垣を背景に侘びた風
情を見せている。地苔も手入れよく青々としている。
亭主の愛情が垣間見えて嬉しい露地である。
MAMIYA R2 180mm F16 1/30 EPR

**92 獨樂庵 露地全景 現代 東京**

獨樂庵は利休好みの二畳の小間であった。再三の移築
をくり返した結果ここ八王子市に落ちついた。移築に
ついて当主は絵図をもとに原型をくずさない努力をし
たといっておられる。灯篭を中心にした山道は遠くて
深い。
SINAR P FUJINON 120mm F22 1/5 EPR

**93 修禅寺 双皎山荘露地全景 現代 静岡**

山の上、梅林の中にこの露地は作られている。露地と
いうよりは書院庭といった感じのほうが強い。書院広
間から見た景観だが関東地方に多いほこりのつきにく
い石材を飛び石に使用し流れを引き込み、飛び石本位
の数奇の庭となっている。
SINAR P FUJINON 90mm F22 1/30 EPR

**94 岡崎氏露地 敷石と中門付近 現代 福岡**

岡崎氏の庭園は山畔に大きな石組を堂々と組み、池泉
を設け、流れを引き、雄大な崖下に露地が営まれてい
る。格調高い敷石の向うに中門があり、それを潜ると
春水庵の茶庭に入る。京風な作りが光っている。
SINAR P FUJINON 120mm F22 1/5 EPR

**95 田中丸氏卍の腰掛待合 現代 福岡**

田中丸邸は市内高台にあり、芝生を中心とした庭園で
ある。広い屋敷の一部に茶室茶庭が点在する。腰掛の
四阿は桂離宮の四阿を忠実に写している。卍形の構成
は貴人腰掛でお互に顔を見合せないよう配慮されてい
る。
SINAR P SUPERANGULON 75mm F11 1/15 EPR

**96 MOA 金の茶室全景 現代 静岡**

茶室を組立て式にして運び歩くという発想は面白い。
また黄金ばかりの茶室を作るというのもまた面白く秀
吉ならではという感じがする。大阪城本丸に置かれた
のがこの写真のような状態であったのであろう。
SINAR P NIKKOR 90mm F11 ストロボ使用 EPR

1 Ginkaku-ji, "Togu-do A Complete View", Muromachi Era (Kyoto)

The official name for the Ginkaku-ji temple is Jisho-ji temple and it was built by Yoshimasa Ashikaga who based the plans on the Kinaku-ji temple which was built by his grandfather, Yoshimitsu. It is said that the Togu-do and Kannon-den (Ginkaku) shown in the picture against the backdrop of Mt. Higashi-yama were constructed with reference to the garden of Saiho-ji temple. The way in which they stand out in the garden with the pond is the personification of beauty.

LINHOF KARDAN SYMMAR 180mm F16/26 1/15 EPR

2 Ginkaku-ji, "A View from Togu-do", Muromachi Era (Kyoto)

On the right-hand side of this family alter room to Buddha lies a statue of Yoshimasa. The blue-stone bridge in the foreground is known as the Senjo bridge and is the oldest part of the whole ponded garden. Behind this alter room is a Doninsai which is famous as being the earliest construction of a study room tea ceremony room.

LINHOF KARDAN FUJINON 120mm F22 1/4 EPR

3 Ginkaku-ji, "Doninsai A Complete View", Muromachi Era (Kyoto)

This is an exterior view of a 4.5-tatami study room, Doninsai. It is said that Yoshimasa built the Togu-do for the special purpose of being a family shrine in which he could worship his ancestors. He must have desired to re-merge the dignity of Jodo of which the principle image was said to be dedicated to Amidha. Lotus blossoms were also planted all around the pond.

LINHOF KARDAN NIKKOR 90mm F11 1/15 EPR

4 Ginkaku-ji, "The Inside of Doninsai", Muromachi Era (Kyoto)

It is known that Doninsai were tea room that originated in a much earlier age, however, owing to the fact that Doninsai were built in the Higashiyama period when the basis of chanoyu was established, it is also possible additional to the tea ceremony. The possibility that Yoshimasa used it as a study in which he occasionally used to drink tea cannot be over-looked.

LINHOF KARDAN SUPERANGULON 75mm F11

5 Daisen-in, "A View from Study Room", Muromachi Era (Kyoto)

This is a Suisho-shitsu, a study room in the Daisen-in which is famous for its Japanese dry garden. It is built along the typical study room style with the floor on the right and the wooden door that is usually kept closed. There is the historical fact that Hideyoshi and Rikyu once had some tea together in this room and that Hideyoshi praised the flower arrangement in the chinkoishi placed in the front of the hall.

SINAR P NIKKOR 90mm F8 1/15 EPR

6 Daisen-in, "A View from Study Room", Muromachi Era (Kyoto)

This is a view from Rei-no-ma. The fact that the wooden and paper door can be removed like a stage setting is interesting and resembles the unique idea of Hideyoshi who fabricated the room and had it carried around with him.

SINAR P SUPERANGULON 75mm F16 1/15 EPR

7 Katsura Rikyu, "Shokin-tei Tea Ceremony Room Washing Water Stone Grouping", Momoyama Era (Kyoto)

There are four tea rooms within Katsura Rikyu. Unlike current tea room which are reserved for the tea ceremony only, these rooms were also used for serving meals and resting. The water font for washing is typical of the general style stone grouping. The water and the stream set in the garden can be likened to the tsukubai.

SINAR P NIKKOR 90mm F11 1/60 EPR

8 Katsura Rikyu, "Shokin-tei Tea Ceremony Room", Momoyama Era (Kyoto)

This is the route to the Shokin-tei. The slightly raised stepping stones lead up to a sloping bridge. A water basin stone grouping similar to that previously mentioned can be seen in the lower right. This particular one was recently restored and gives an additional beauty. It stands out with its shining water surface.

SINAR P SUPERANGULON 75mm F11 1/15 EPR

9 Katsura Rikyu, "Koshikake Waiting Bench", Momoyama Era (Kyoto)

This is a koshikake waiting room in the Shokin-tei. A gigantic Japanese fern palm can be seen just in front of the seat. Fern palms such as this were commonly seen in gardens of this period. The dual measuring-cup shaped water basins set on the far left and the stepping stones stretching from right to left draw the whole thing together.

SINAR P SUPERANGULON 75mm F11 1/15 EPR

10 Katsura Rikyu, "Koshikake Waiting Bench Suna-setchin", Momoyama Era (Kyoto)

All tea garden are possessed of suna setchin and shita-hara setchin. Setchin is a toilet, but it was considered a kind of courtesy for guests to take a look inside. The inside is uniquely laid out with the stone grouping, foot-rest and white sand. Shitahara setchin is a real toilet.

SINAR P ANGULON 75mm F16 1sec. EPR

11 Omote Senke, "Fushin-an Nakakuguri (Wicket Gate)", Momoyama Era (Kyoto)

There are outer roji and inner roji in this tea garden. Nakakuguri is located in the centre of these and serves as a main gate. Although it reportedly did not exist druing the Rikyu period, I believe it did. Like the nijiriguchi entrance to the tea room, it was designed in the common style to cause people to crouch as they entered.

LINHOF KARDAN SUPERANGULON 75mm F16 1/2 EPR

12 Omote Senke, "Fushin-an Baiken-mon Gate and Yakuishi", Momoyama Era (Kyoto)

This is the yakuishi and the middle gate leading to Fushin-an. This is where a host and a guest met for the first time to exchange a few words. A few steps through this gate would find words. A few steps through this gate would find the koshikake waiting room on the right and the Fushin-an a little further along the stepping stones. The simple and quiet taste of this area is filled with a kind of tension and cutting.

LINHOF KARDAN SUPERANGULON 75mm F16 1sec. EPR

13 Omote Senke, "Fushin-an Koshikake Waiting Bench A Complete View", Momoyama Era (Kyoto)
Guests are seated here while they await their turn to center the tea room. The time of waiting is full of strong expectations. It is also the moment when the hearts of guests are swollen and stimulated by the thought of the oncoming tea ceremony. The beautifully streaming water dashed on the stepping stones purifies the area.
LINHOF KARDAN NIKKOR 90m F22 1/4 EPR

14 Omote Senke, "Fushin-an Roji A Complete View", Momoyama Era (Kyoto)
Roji in tea garden is the space surrounding the tea room with mountains, rivers, valleys and mountain-paths which are rendolent of typical Japanese scenery. The thick growth of the plants could be the forest and the stepping stones the animals. The path with its gentle slope could be the hill. This has to be the most typical of tea gardens.
LINHOF KARDAN NIKKOR 90mm F22 1/2 EPR

15 Jo-an, "A Complete View", Momoyama Era (Aichi)
Uraku Oda was the younger brother of Nobunaga. After the death of Nobunaga he placed his loyalty in the hands of Hideyoshi and turned to religion. This tea room, known as Jo-an Uraku, was moved many times before it eventually settled on its current location in Oyama city. It is also known as Koyomi-no-seki. It features the entrance for nobility and the nijiriguchi entrance to the tea room in a combination of styles from soan and shoin.
SINAR P NIKKOR 90mm F11 1/20 EPR

16 Jo-an, "Around the Izutsu", Momoyama Era (Aichi)
Good water is indispensable for tea making and a well is therefore essential for all tea gardens. They are gilded with stones or bored into the shape of circles or squares. This well is named "Samegai" and has the name Uraku and the date engraved on it.
SINAR P SYMMAR 150mm F22 1/2 EPR

17 Urasenke, "Yuin A Complete View", Edo Era (Kyoto)
This is one of the typical tea gardens of Urasenke, which literally means "To hide again". Sen Sotan yields ownership of Fushin-an to Koshin Soza, the grandson of Rikyu, and entrusted Senso Soshitsu to run Konnichi-an while he took care of this Yuin. It is said that the stones known as the scattered bean stones in front of the nijiriguchi entrance were unintentionally placed there by Sotan himself.
SINAR P NIKKOR 90mm F22 1sec. EPR

18 Urasenke, "Yuin Tsukubai" Edo Era (Kyoto)
This is the water basin treasured by the late Rikyu. It is improved by the stony-tower trend of the Kamakura Era, and forms a beautiful shape with the figures of the engraved Buddhas all around it. The production of a deep and hidden taste for the quiet and simple which has been created by the surrounding plants is admirable.
SINAR P NIKKOR 90mm F2 1sec. EPR

19 Urasenke, "Around The Sarudo", Edo Era (Kyoto)
This area cerates the atmosphere of a meeting taking place between a host and his guest at this very moment while walking through the deep mountains. It has been said from olden times that the saruto was built by Rikyu, the nakakuguri based on an idea by Oribe, and the middle gate built by Enshu. The water-sprinkled yakuishi is beautiful.
SINAR P NIKKOR 90mm F22 1sec. EPR

20 Urasenke, "Koshikake Waiting Bench and Yakuishi", Edo Era (Kyoto)
This is a koshikake waiting room set in front of the Mushiki-ken. A kijinishi is laid on the far left of this koshikake, and other guest stones are in the form of block stones like long stepping stones. The neighbouring yakuishi possesses such dignity and status that one cannot help but admire it. The shape of the dust hole positioned by the broom in the roji on the bottom right is increadible.
SINAR P SUPERANGULON 77mm F22 5sec. reflex

21 Koho-an, "Bosen Around the Roketsu Water Basin", Edo Era (Kyoto)
Daitoku-ji temple and chanoyu have a very intimate relationship owing to people like Juko Murata, Rikyu and the Buddhist priest Ikkyu. Above all, the construction of the Koho-an Bosen tea room set in the Bodai-ji temple in Enshu excels all others. The idea of changing the view by arranging the four panelless paper-doors in different positions is out of this world.
LINHOF KARDAN SUPERANGULON 90mm F22 1/4 EPR

22 Koho-an, "The Inside of Bosen", Edo Era (Kyoto)
Koho-an was originally founded by Enshu Kobori within the site of the Ryuko-in and transfered to its present site in 1643. It was restored by the aids of the Konoe family, Fumi to Matsudaira and others, after it was destroyed by fire. The stepping stones set in the site were damaged by the fire, but it is said that they have been kept like this since the Enshu period.
LINHOF KARDAN FUJINON 120mm F22 1/8 EPR

23 Koho-an, "Sanunjo Sword Hanger and Hanger Stones", Edo Era (Kyoto)
Owing to the rule that there should not be any discrimination between noble men, samurai and town folk during the tea ceremony, samurai were not allowed to carry around their swords within the area. Because of this they came up with the idea of setting up this sannunjo sword hanging stone. It is a pretrified tree with an age stretching through the centuries and its surface pattern closely resembles that of a cut tree.
LINHOF KARDAN NIKKOR 90mm F22 1/2 EPR

24 Shugakuin Rikyu, "Kyutsui-tei A Complete View", Edo Era (Kyoto)
The tea houses in Shugakuin Rikyu, are set on three different levels. The Kyutsui-tei is located in Nakajima, the highest place that commands the best view. With its view of northern Kyoto and Nishiyama through the Yokuryu pond, it can be considered to be a first class example of a Japanese garden. The autumn tint adds to its beauty.
SINNAR P NIKKOR 90mm F16 1/60 EPR

25 Shugakuin Rikyu, "The Inside of Kyutsui-tei", Edo Era (Kyoto)
The Shugakuin was run by the Tokugawa clan from Omizuya-in. This house was especially constructed with a large space and high ceilings in the west and north to provide good views. The part that rises one floor above the others in the centre of the photograph was the seat for the ex-emperor. The work in the frame was actually done by the ex-emperor himself.
SINAR P SUPERANGULON 75mm F11 1sec. EPR

26 Shugakuin Rikyu, "Jugetsukancha-tei", Edo Era (Kyoto)
The Jugetsukan tea house is located at the foot of the mountain and was sited for Omizuya-in. It was restored to its original condition during the Bunsei Era. At the very front stands a water conduit. The faint sound of the water coming from the mouth of the waterfall produces an atmosphere that seems to belong to another world. The framed picture of Jugestukan is also the work of the exemperor.
LINHOF KARDAN NIKKOR 90mm F22 1/2 EPR

27 Shugakuin Rikyu, "Jugetsukan Stepping Stones", Edo Era (Kyoto)
This is a view of the stepping-stones from the upper hall. The pleasantly shaped stepping stones curve off to the right at the forked junction. Keeping straight to this will bring you to the sawawatariishi. The triangle shape along the path was made to resemble Mt. Fuji. This path will then continue onto the mouth of the waterfall called Shiraito-no-taki.
LINHOF KARDAN NIKKOR 90mm F22 1/15 EPR

28 Yabunouchi Soke, "En-an Around The Nijiriguchi", Edo Era (Kyoto)
Yabunouchi Soke was the house of a tea ceremony teacher from the Nishi Hongan-ji temple and is built along samurai lines in the style of Shoin. Kenchu, the founder, married the younger sister of Oribe, which related them by marriage. Consideration for people of nobility is prominent in this roji. A good example is the koshikake waiting room.
LINHOF KARDAN NIKKOR 90mm F22 1/2 EPR

29 Yabunouchi Soke, "En-an Tsukubai Mongakuishi Water Basin", Edo Era (Kyoto)
This water basin was a fabrication of a gorin-to (a gravestone composed of five pieces piled on top of one another) from the Kamakura Era. The name of the basin was taken from Mongaku as this gorin-to was situated on the site of his residence. Many water basins were made of stone and represented various ornamental shapes such as lanterns, foundations, bridge stakes and temple towers, etc.
LINHOF KARDAN NIKKOR 150mm F22 1/2 EPR

30 Yabunouchi Soke, "Teppo-gaki and Stepping Stones", Edo Era (Kyoto)
The formation of the stepping stones leading to the roji entrance from the En-an is beautiful. A nishino-ya lantern can be viewed in the far distance. A walk along the Teppo-gaki summons up mental pictures of a noble man with a fine stride out for a walk with his page. But this is only my imagination.
LINHOF KARDAN NIKKOR 90mm F22 1/4 EPR

31 Ninna-ji, "Hito-tei Around the Kijinguchi and Sword Hanger", Edo Era (Kyoto)
Ninna-ji temple is the temple of the Imperial priest. The Hito-tei viewed across the pond is the tea room for people of the nobility which was dearly loved by the lake Emperor Kokaku. The fossilized hanger stone and sword hanger on the right are more placid and comfortably spacious than the fossilized ones used in the Soan style tea rooms.
LINHOF KARDAN SUPERANGULON 75mm F16 1/25 EPR

32 Ninna-ji, "Hito-tei A Complete View", Edo Era (Kyoto)
There are two prominent tea arbours in the Ninna-ji temple. They are the Hito-tei and the Ryokaku-tei. A wander through the deep forest with its view of the stone bridge over the Soan style running stream in front of the Ryokaku-tei and the view of the beautiful kijinguchi entrance beyond the mountain stream with its stepping stones which spread out from amongst the trees makes one feel that one has finally reached the mountain cottage.
LINHOF KARDAN SYMMAR 150mm F22 1/2 EPR

33 Ninna-ji, "The Inside of Hito-tei", Edo Era (Kyoto)
The circular window on the right is supposed to represent the sun rising out of the ocean at Hito. With this in mind, it is easy to imagine. The earth-packed floor is known as a Horadoko. It was designated as a national treasure in 1937 and as an important cultural property in 1952.
LINHOF KARDAN NIKKOR 75mm F11 flash EPR

34 Kodai-ji, "Karakasa-tei A Complete View", Edo Era (Kyoto)
It is said that Karakasa-tei in the precinct of Kodai-ji temple was transfered from Fushimi Castle. It is also said that Karakasa-tei was Rikyu's favourite tea house although there is no proof of this. It is famous for its unique shape created by the passage linking it with neighbouring Shigure-tei.
SINAR P SYMMAR 150mm F22 1/30 EPR

35 Kodai-ji, "Inside of Karakasa-tei, Edo Era (Kyoto)
I wonder whose idea it was to attach the names Karakasa-tei and Shigure-tei for these two connected structures which resemble the shape of an umbrella? The way in which the dressing attic spreads out like the spokes of a wheel in both interesting and unique.
LINHOF KARDAN SUPERANGULON 75mm F8 flash EPR

36 Rokuso-an, "A Complete View (Tokyo National Museum)", Edo Era (Tokyo)
The Imperial Museum bought this tea house from its original site in Jigen-in, Kofuku-ji temple in Nara and restored it within this building. It is said that Rokuso-an was constructed in the style favoured by Sowa Kanamori. There are many cases where tea houses have survived owing to having been transfered in this way.
SINAR P FUJINON 120mm F11 1/15 EPR

37 Rokuso-an, "Around The Tsukubai", Edo Era (Tokyo)
I have seen many types of Tsukubai in tea gardens, and in many cases the bamboo tube is used to pour the water as is being done in this picture. It is more common in the Kanto Plain. During the tea ceremony the host would bring in the water and clean it while awaiting the arrival of the guest. In this case, the tsukubai is mostly used as an ornament for the tea garden.
LINHOF KARDAN NIKKOR 180mm F22 1/2 EPR

38 Shoka-do, "Tea Ceremony Room A Complete View", Edo Era (Kyoto)
This is the tea hall of Shokado. It is a thatched hermitage in the form of a small living quarter of two tatemi mats, a household Buddhist alter, a portable washing area, a small cupboard and an earthen furnace. The colorful picture of the sun and the Chinese Pheonix on the ceiling is breathtaking in contrast to the plain exterior.
LIMHOF KARDAN SUPERANGULON 75mm F16 1/4 EPR

39 Shoka-do, "A Corner to Study Room Flagestones", Edo Era (Kyoto)
Shoka-do roji was transfered from Iwashimizu Hachiman-gu with its garden of Senbo and restored in its current location. Many alterations were made to the garden, but the neighbouring area of the tea house seems to have kept its original appearance beautifully.
LINHOF KARDAN FUJINON 120mm F22 1/2 EPR

40 Saio-in, "Around the Middle Gate", Edo Era (Kyoto)
Saio-in is a minor temple of the Komei-ji and is famous as one of the works of Yoken Fujimura along with the Mr. Izone's Tennenzuga-tei tea garden in Shiga. The vicinity of the central gate set in the outer roji as shown in this picture is pleasantly neat and tidy.
SINAR P SYMMAR 150mm F22 1/15 EPR

41 Saio-in, "Yodomi-seki Around the Nijiriguchi", Edo Era (Kyoto)
Yoken Fujimura was one of the disciples of Sen Sotan and one of the big four than mastered the art of Senke. Owing to the fact that the tea house stands of the north-western hill, this Saio-in used to provide a distant view of Yodo and Yamazaki and the seki therefore became to be known as Yodomi-seki.
SINAR P NIKKOR 90mm F22 1/15 EPR

42 Saio-in, "Yodomi-seki Kesa-gata Tsukubai", Edo Era (Kyoto)
This is a Kesa-gata water basin set in front of the nijiriguchi entrance of Yokomi-seki. Usually a Tsukubai would be shaped like a lantern, etc., but this was the exception. It is sturdily set beneath the white cedar (hinoki) that was planted by Yoken. The formation of the stones are quite beautiful with the waku stone on the right, the teshoku (candlestick) stone on the left and the yakuishi at the front.
SINAR P NIKKOR 150mm F22 1/15 EPR

43 Koto-in, "Shoko-ken Around the Tsukubai", Edo Era (Kyoto)
Koto-in was founded by Sansai Hosokawa to hold masses for the repose of his father, Yusai's soul. The lantern brought from Rikyu is worshipped in the precinct as Sansai's grave. The name of the tea ceremony was associated with the tea house that was created in the vicinity of the Eko pine tree in front of the Kitano library of Buddhist sutras at the time of the Kitano tea party. A frame with the characters "Shoko" written in it hangs on the wall of the room.
LINHOF KARDAN SUPERANGULON 75mm F22 2sec. EPR

44 Koto-in, "Shoko-ken Around the Nijiriguchi", Edo Era (Kyoto)
This is a tsukubai set in front of the Shoko-ken. The Oribe lantern proudly shows off its chunky existance in this rural area. By the bold way that the front stone has been placed one can imagine that it was arranged by a man with skill. The moderately planted grove produces an excellent atmosphere of the hermitage style roji.
LINHOF KARDAN FUJINON 120mm F22 2sec. EPR.

45 Mr. Izome's Tennenzuga-tei, "Front Garden", Edo Era (Shiga)
In the vicinity of Fumi-do along the old highway stands the residence of Katada, the leader of Katada's surface force who served as the village headsman through a successive generation. The styles of Shoin and roji gardens are well blended in this garden to produce a simpleness. On a clear day it affords a distant view of Mt. Omi Fuji.
SINAR P FUJINON 120mm F22 1/60 EPR

46 Mr. Izome's Tennenzuga-tei, "Tachitsukubai", Edo Era (Shiga)
This large vertical flagstone practically jumps out at you when visiting the area where this well-shaped Tachi-tsukubai stands. This typical construction of Shoin and roji styles was said to be the joint work of Yoken Fujimura and Yuan Kitamura. This typical Tachi-tsukubai flanked by the pail stone on the right and candlestick stone on the left stands out perfectly in the garden.
SINAR P SYMMAR 150mm F22 1/30 EPR

47 Mr. Nishida's Gyokusen-en, "Around the Study Room Fumiwake Stepping Stones", Edo Era (Ishikawa)
These are stepping stones laid out in front of the study room in the west garden. The larger stones set out in this garden are rather low for the snow country. The large stone in the centre is one of the stepping stones and gently leads off to the right. On the right of this stands a tsukubai with a picture of eulalia engraved on it. It is a fine and dignified stone-work tsukubai.
SINAR P NIKKOR 90mm F22 1/2 EPR

48 Mr. Nishida's Gyokusen-en, "East Garden Around the Well", Edo Era (Ishikawa)
Gyokusen-en is the east garden that commands a view of the forest in Kenroku-en which is famous for being the private garden of the feudal lords of Kaga Castle town. The stepping stones that are laid out beside this garden lead to the Saisetsu-tei. This harshly built well looks strong and sturdy. A well is an indespensible part of the tea ceremony.
SINAR P FUJINON 120mm 1sec. EPR

**49 Mr. Nishida's Gyokusen-en,** "Kanun-tei Stepping Stones", Edo Era (Ishikawa)

These are stepping stones laid out in front of the Kanun-tei. The Kanun-tei is found amongst the tea houses of Urasenke. This Shoin-style tea house was said to be one of Sotan's favourites. Mr. Nishida's Kanun-tei is a copy, so this group of stepping stones have a placid and dignified air.
SINAR P SIMMAR 150mm F22 1/2 EPR

**50 Mr. Nishida's Gyokusen-en,** "Main Garden Fumiwake Stepping Stones and Middle Gate", Edo Era (Ishikawa)

Chisen (pond and spring) Garden is located off to the right side in the Gyokusen-en; the low sound of a waterfall is heard from afar above the mountains. This is a strolling garden of the early Edo Era. We come to the Saisetsu-tei bower on top of the mountain after passing the middle gate following these stepping stones. The landscape begins to look more like a country inn of this area.
SINAR P FUJINON 120mm F22 1/2 EPR

**51 Mr. Nishida's Gyokusen-en,** "Saisetsu-tei and Stepping Stones", Edo Era (Ishikawa)

This garden was completed over four generations starting from Wakita Naokata, the first founder. The second founder, Naoyoshi is said to have guided the Saisetsu-tei roji because he was a disciple to Senso Soshitsu. The design of the wide overhang of the eaves and high stepping stones for deep snow befits snow country.
SINAR P FUJINON 90mm F22 1/2 EPR

**52 Juko-an,** "Tsukubai (Shomyo-ji", Edo Era (Nara)

The tea house in the Shomyo-ji temple in Nara is said to have connections with Murata Juko. Juko served Yoshimasa Ashikaga and learned Zen from a Zen priest, Ikkyu. He is credited with the origination of "soan cha", unifying the tea ceremony and Zen. The stone basin has an unusually large water hole apparently for practicality.
SINAR P FUJINON 120mm F16 1/30 EPR

**53 Juko-an,** "A Complete View (Shomyo-Ji)", Edo Era (Nara)

A large entrance for noble people is located at the front. However, the shoe-taking-off stone is small and a wet edge is also provided, which gives an impression of nonchalance. Also the sword hanging stone is small and the sword hanger is moderate in size. Am I the only one who thinks that this may be the mind of Juko, and originator of the tea ceremony?
SINAR P SUPERANGULON 75mm F16 1/2 EPR

**54 Jiko-in,** "Study Room A Distant View", Edo Era (Nahara)

The thatched roof of the "Irimoya-zukuri" looks more like a country house than a study room. This is a vista point for the Tomio River flowing nearby. This is a tea house which the Governor of Katagiri Iwami-no-kami Sadamasa, the originator of the Sekishu School, liked. A very open and generous mind of a warrior is apparent.
MAMIYA R2 SEKOR 150mm F16 1/30 EPR

**55 Jiko-in,** "The Inside of Tea Ceremony Room", Edo Era (Nara)

The view from the upper room of the study room is wonderful. The borrowed scenery largely taking in the mountains of Nara develops a panoramic view harmonizing with the large bushes in the garden. This picture shows floor seating in the "nijodaime" and attached two-tatami-mat waiting room which Sekishu is said to have like very much.
LINHOF KARDAN SUPERANGULON 75mm flash EPR

**56 Kosho-ji,** "Roji Tsukubai", Edo Era (Kyoto)

The tomb of Oribe Furuta is in the Kosho-ji temple. Oribe was a high disciple of Rikyu, but his tastes run almost contrary to those of his master Rikyu. In the Oribe School, the tea bowl comes on a stand even if the tea should be weak. The heavy "Garan" stone against the background of the Oribe stone lantern befits a Daimyo's stone basin.
SINAR P FUJINON 120mm F22 1sec. EPR

**57 Toyo-bo,** "Roji A Complete View", Edo Era (Kyoto)

This is a famous tea house located in the main building of Kennin-ji temple, which is the headquarters of the sect. Toyo-bo was an expert in tea ceremony in Rikyu's school and was the chief priest of Toyo-bo in the precinct of Shinnyo-do Hall. It is said that he built this tea house on the bank of the Kamiya River on the occasion of the Kitano grand tea ceremony, but this is not certain.
SINAR P NIKKOR 90mm F22 f1/10 EPR

**58 Kankyu-an,** "Koshikake Waiting Bench", Edo Era (Kyoto)

The name Kankyu-an can be interpreted in two ways. It is interpreted either that the first founder, Ichio, suspended his official work when he resigned his position or that one devotes himself in the tea ceremony detached from daily life. Isn't it a name which gives us a strong impression of thinking that is a little extreme?
SINAR P NIKKOR 90mm F22 1/2 EPR

**59 Kankyu-an,** "Around the Nijiriguchi", Edo Era (Kyoto)

Ichio Munemori, the first founder of Mushanokoji Senke, was born the second son of Sen Sotan. He is said to have built this tea house in 1667 when he retired from government service for the Takamatsu Provinces. The sode-gaki on the eastern side of the nijiriguchi stepping stones adds a taste of a Wabi-soan. The dust hole beyond the stepping stones also adds a taste of the countryside.
SINAR P SUPERANGULON 75mm F22 3sec. EPR

**60 Kankyu-an,** "Kansui-en Garanishi Water Basin", Edo Era (Kyoto)

Kansui-ken is a Mushanokoji Senke style tea house. The water basin placed in front of it has the beautiful form of a garanishi. The very low position of the teokeishi and teshokuishi keystones is very characteristic.
LINHOF KARDAN FUJINON 120mm 1/2 EPR

**61 Kankyu-an,** "Middle Gate Stepping Stones and Waiting Bench", Edo Era (Kyoto)

Stepping stones in front of the Amigasa-mon (middle gate); Fumiwake stones are seen in the middle. Nokkoshi stones of the garan stones are seen under the middle gate. It was planned to lead the guest to the waiting bench as he walks straight toward the tea house from the middle gate following the stepping stones. The landscape, provided with running water, puts us in another world.
SINAR P NIKKOR 90mm F22 1sec. EPR

**62 Kankyu-an,** "Tomeishi", Edo Era (Kyoto)

A Tomeishi is in front of the waiting bench. It is also called the Sekimoriishi. It is placed at the junction of stepping stones of the roji to limit the passage of the guest. It is an implicit sign that you cannot go beyond it. It is also sometimes to add scenic beauty to the roji.
SINAR P NIKKOR 210mm F22 1/2 EPR

**63 Kenroku-en,** "Yugao-tei A Complete View", Edo Era (Ishikawa)

The Kenroku-en garden is one of the three major gardens in Japan. There is a tea house in Samurai style, Yabunouchi En-an style, in front of the Hisago Pond in the garden. It is called the Yugao-tei. It is also called the Takimi-tei, since there is a big waterfall just in front of it. The "domahi" inside the eaves is deep to befit snow country. The "hokei-zukuri" design has a beautiful form.
SINAR P NIKKOR 90mm F22 1/15 EPR

**64 Kenroku-en,** "The Inside of Yugao-tei", Edo Era (Ishikawa)

The entrances located in three directions lead to the nijiriguchi to the south, the nobleman's entrance to the west and the guest seat to the north. The vermilion wall is beautiful. The landscape with the view of setting sun from the house is wonderful. We feel that this is truly a tea house for noblemen.
SINAR P SUPERANGULON 75mm F16 flash

**65 Kenroku-en,** "Yugao-tei Kantan Water Basin", Edo Era (Ishikawa)

There is a round water basin edging with a deep "domahi" in three directions. It is called the Kanatan water basin, since an anecdote of Kantan's dream is inscribed on the upper part of water hole. It is a work by a metalworker, named Teijo Goto, of the early Edo Era.
SINAR P FUJINON 120 mm F22 1/2 EPR

**66 Keishun-in,** "Study Room Stepping Stones and Sarudo", Edo Era (Kyoto)

The Keishun-in in the precinct of Myoshin-ji temple has a tea house called the Kaihaku-an and an attached garden. Having a deep relationship with Yoken Fujimura, the chief priest of the Myosho-ji temple is instructing tea ceremony as a master of the Yoken School even now. The roji is separated into upper and lower parts. The picture shows the upper part of the roji in the Kaihaku-an.
SINAR P NIKKOR 90mm F22 1/25 EPR

**67 Keishun-in,** "Hojo East Garden Stepping Stones and Flagstones", Edo Era (Kyoto)
A view of the Baiken-mon gate viewed from the eastern garden of the lower "hojo". The "ooarare-shiki-nobedan" on the near side leads to the "hojo". The scenery around here makes us feel as if we are walking on a mountain road because of its many plants. However, the style of an ordinary garden and that of a roji are undiscernibly mixed.
SINIAR P FUJINON 120mm F22 1/15 EPR

**68 Jodo-ji,** "Roteki-an A Complete View", Edo Era (Hiroshima)
Jodo-ji temple in Onomichi City in Hiroshima Prefecture is an old temple which is said to have been founded by Prince Shotoku. This is a tea house favored by Hideyoshi Toyotomi and it was moved from Fushimi Castle. This is an En-an style tea house and reflects a style that Oribe liked. Refined stepping stones are comfortably placed and add a touch of elegance.
SINAR P NIKKOR 90mm F22 1/15 EPR

**69 Jodo-ji,** "Roteki-an Waiting Bench", Edo Era (Hiroshima)
This is a waiting bench giving strong impressions. This waiting bench for noblemen is full of a light, vivid feeling. The nobleman's stone on the left side is placed in a little higher place and the guest's stone is a cut stone. The lattice above the guest's seat slides horizontally; the light from the exterior is shaded if it is slid to the right or to the left.
SINAR P NIKKOR 90mm F22 1/30 EPR

**70 Komon-do,** "Roji Koshikake Waiting Bench", Edo Era (Shimane)
This is a roji tea house in the Renjo-in in the precinct of Shimizu-ji temple in Yasuki City in Shimane Prefecture. It was built in the beginning of the 19th century by Totsukoan Eikyo, the chief priest of this temple. Priest Eikyo had learned at the Sansai Hosokawa School. This tea house was built with old timber from the main gate of Shimizu-ji temple, salvaged on the occasion of repairing the temple's precinct. So this house has come to be called the Komon-do, according to the legend. This picture shows a waiting bench probably intended for noblemen. The nobleman's seat is on the left side. The guest's seat is equipped with a round cushion and a cigar tray for waiting guests.
MAMIYA R2 SEKOR 50mm~105mm F11~22 1/30~1/2

**71 Komon-do,** "Around the Nijiriguchi", Edo Era (Shimane)
This is a nijiriguchi. The outstanding stepping stones are impressive. The sword hanging stone is small and gives an impression of "bun-jin".
MAMIY R2 SEKOR 50mm~105mm F11~22 1/30~1/2

**72 Komon-do,** "Roji Flagstones", Edo Era (Shimane)
Old roof tiles are used as the roji flagstones. The standing stone basin is provided with a washbowl. This is a view in front of the decorative pot.
MAMIYA R2 SEKOR 50mm~105mm F11~22 1/30~1/2

**73 Komon-do,** "Around the Kijinguchi", Edo Era (Shimane)
This is an entrance for noblemen. The nonchalant mood is amiable. The scene across the yotsume-gaki hedge also shows a taste of "bun-jin".
MAMIYA R2 SEKOR 50mm~105mm F11~22 1/30~1/2

**74 Komon-do,** "Taki Stone Grouping", Edo Era (Shimane)
The Komon-do has "o-daki" (male) and "me-daki" (female) waterfalls. This is a scene of the stepping stones in front of the male waterfall. A gentle mood can be felt.
MAMIYA R2 SEKOR 50mm~105mm F11~22 1/30~1/2

**75 Komon-do,** "Tea Ceremony Room Viewed from the Waterfall", Edo Era (Shimane)
The tea ceremony room is located beyond the yotsume-gaki in the front. The scene around here shows a bush reminding one of a roji.
MAMIYA R2 SEKOR 50mm~105mm F11~22 1/30~1/2

**76 Hassou-an,** "A Complete View", Edo Era (Nara)
The Hasso-an was moved to its present location in 1892 from the garden of the Daijo-in of Kofuku-ji temple. It used to be called the Gansui-tei. Oribe Furuta is said to have liked it. The swoed hanging stone leading to the nijiriguchi inside the eaves from the rather large stepping stone in the middle of the line of stepping stones in the front is small and gentle.
SINAR P NIKKOR 180mm F22 1/30 EPR

**77 Gyokurin-in,** "Sa-an Roji A Complete View", Edo Era (Kyoto)
A tea ceremony room in the Gyokurin-in of Daitoku-ji temple. It is attached to the mortuary table hall Nanmyo-an built by Ryoei Konoike, a millionaire in Osaka. It was completed under the guidance of Joshinsai, the seventh headmaster of the Omote Senke School. The flagstones of "oararejiki" are covered with ground moss, which is so beautiful that you feel guilty stepping on them.
LINHOF KARDAN NIKKOR 90mm F22 1/15 EPR

**78 Sankei-en,** "Konmokutsu A Complete View", Meiji Era (Kanagawa)
Tomitaro Hara called himself Sankei Hara. He was born in a rich farmer's house in Gifu and succeeded in business. He then created a large garden in Hommoku of Yokohama to satisfy his predilection for old art. The Konmokutsu is a tea ceremony room which the old Sankei loved best. Its name derives from the wood of the high beam of Daitoku-ji temple's main gate used in it.
LINHOF KARDAN NIKKOR 90mm F22 1/2 EPR

**79 Sankei-en,** "Shunsoro A Complete View", Meiji Era (Kanagawa)
A tea ceremony room originally located in the Mimuro-do Konzo-in in Uji. It was transferred to Sankei-en in 1918. It has 9 windows, which give the tea room the other name of the Kyuso-tei (Nine-window Bower). There is an impressive "garan" stone on the right side of the roji shown in the picture and a stone basin on the left side. The rustic washbowl dug in the natural stone is elegant.
LINHOF KARDAN NIKKOR 90mm F22 1/2 EPR

**80 Rokasensui-so,** "Shako-tei Around the Well", Taisho Era (Shiga)
The residence of Shunkyo Yamamoto, a famous painter in the Japanese art world of Kyoto. He planned and supervised the construction of this garden himself. I like this planting of "susuki" very much. Whenever I come here to visit him, I find the "susuki" trees to have grown in the same manner and to the same height. I am pleased with the master's mind in tea ceremony, evident in his care the garden.
LINHOF KARDAN NIKKOR 28mm F22 1/30 EPR

**81 Rokasensui-so,** "Kion-do Tsukubai", Taisho Era (Shiga)
There is a "Yohobutsu" washbowl in the shape of the "nakabachi" style. The "nakabachi" style is a manner that edging is provided to surround the stone basin at the center. This "nakabachi" style is also found in the tsukubai of the headmaster of the Matsuo School mentioned earlier. A framing to make a stone art object look better.
LINHOF KARDAN FUJINON 180mm F22 1/15 EPR

**82 Kobori Soke,** "Roji A Night View", Present Age (Tokyo)
The Seishu-an roji of the headmaster of the Enshu Soke School in Shinano-machi, Tokyo. The "Shirakawa" sand, mound and ground moss on a narrow strip of land look very beautiful and there is a stream along the center of the garden. A low shiori-do yotsume-gaki marks the boundary. This picture is a scene at night. An other-worldly realm has been created.
LINHOF KARAN NIKKOR 90mm F11 8sec.~20sec.

**83 Kobori Soke,** "Tsukubai Viewed from the Nijiriguchi", Present Age (Tokyo)
The tea garden stone basin of the 12th headmaster who is a direct descendent of Enshu Kobori, a daimyo and tea master of the early Edo Era. The water basin of natural stone conjures up an atmosphere of "soan". The contrast of the hand lantern stone on the left and the front stone is harmonious for neatness.
LINHOF KARDAN NIKKOR 90mm F22 1/2 EPR

84 Tea Ceremony Association (Dainihon Chado Gakkai), "Around the Baiken-mon Gate", Present Age (Tokyo)

Sensho Tanaka, founder of the Dainihon Chado Gakkai, blew fresh air into the tea ceremony meeting under his idea that there is no school in tea ceremony. He came to Kyoto to study and stayed at Zuisetsu Maeda's. He received the most profound teaching from Konnichi-an. The picture is a view of the middle gate from the eastern edge of the Kainanken.
SINAR P NIKKOR 90mm F22 1/2 EPR

85 Tea Ceremony Association (Dainihon Chado Gakkai), "Tsukubai", Present Age (Tokyo)

The water basin using the body of the "hoto" which is the stone basin in front of the tea ceremony room "Chisui-tei" is unpretentious as are the keystones around it. It also gives off a quiet feeling. The hexagonal stone lantern behind looks quite like the one of the Kitanotenman-gu Shrine. It creates a world of humbleness together with the deep planting.
SINAR P FUJINON 120mm F22 1sec. EPR

86 Mr. Matsuo's Roji, "Around the Shiorido", Present Age (Aichi)

This is a tea garden of the headmaster of the Matsuo Tea Ceremony School. It represents the tastes of the 10th headmaster Fusensai. The tea garden and the tea ceremony room were completed in 1953. The "Shoin-tei" is located beyond a narrow roji from the main building's guest room. The keystones near the shiori-do are arranged as usual to create a "soan"-like atmosphere.
LINHOF KARDAN NIKKOR 90mm F22 1/10 EPR

87 Mr. Matsuo's Roji, "Tsukubai", Present Age (Aichi)

The stone basin of the "Shoin-tei" of the Matsuo School. This picture was taken from the nijiriguchi. The cylindrical washbowl has a beautiful form. A wide part is allocated for the well of the basin for grandness as well as a large stone being placed boldly in the front. The low arrangement of the "yuokeishi" and the high arrangement of the hand lantern stone are reasonable.
LINHOF KARDAN NIKKOR 90mm F22 1/2 EPR

88 Mr. Yoshida's Roji, "Around the Baiken-mon Gate", Present Age (Aichi)

The Yoshida family has been succeeding the Omote Senke School in Nagoya. Granted mastery by Sokuchusai Soza in 1949, the Yoshida family is one of the most prestigious representing the tea ceremony school. The inconspicuous arrangement of stepping stones near the Baiken-mon gate is humble and tentle. There is a koshikake waiting bench to the left front of the gate.
SINAR P NIKKOR 90mm F22 1/5 PER

89 Mr. Yoshida's Roji, "Around the Tsukubai", Present Age (Aichi)

This roji was created by the last headmaster Akimura around 1949 or 1950. The stone basin was from the "Ankan-tei" and has the design of "niho-gatte". As it is indicated in the name, the stonework can be used from the near side as well as from the far side. Keystones are also arranged so that guests use the stone devices face to face.
SINAR P FUJINON 120mm F22 1/2 EPR

90 Mr. Ozawa's Roji, "A Complete View", Present Age (Miyagi)

The Ozawa Residence is owned by an old family in the Tohoku District. The owner family is now running a hospital. The main entrance gate is a feature to appreciate. This tea room is located to the left of the main building behind the gate. When I visited the place — it was in fall — gingko tree leaves were shining gold in the setting sun. The designer was Masahisa Koyama, a high disciple of Mirei Shigemori.
SINAR P NIKKOR 90mm F11 1/60 EPR

91 Mr. Ozawa's, "Tsukubai and Koets-gaki", Present Age (Miyagi)

A coin-shaped water basin with a square hole at its center and an "ike-komi" style stone lantern, both of which were designed by Masahisa Koyama, combine to create the ambience of "wabi" against the backdrop of a "koetsu-gaki" hedge. Moss on the ground is green. This roji is pleasant to look at because the master likes and takes good care of the garden.
MAMIYA R2 180mm F16 1/30 EPR

92 Dokuraku-an, "Roji A Complete View", Present Age (Tokyo)

The Dokuraku-an is a small tea house with two tatami mats showing the taste of Rikyu. Being moved so often, the Dokuraku-an has finally settled at its present location in Hachioji, Tokyo. The owner says that efforts were made not to alter the original shape, referring to old drawings. Mountain roads running through stone lanterns are deep and reach far.
SINAR P FUJINON 120mm F22 1/5 EPR

93 Shuzen-ji, "Sokosanso Roji A Complete View", Present Age (Shizuoka)

This roji was created in a plum-tree grove on top of a mountain. It looks more like a study room garden than a roji. This is a view from the study room. The stone, which hardly gathers dust, is often used as a material for stepping stones in the Kanto District. A stream was led in. This is a quaint-looking garden in which the stepping stones play the central role.
SINAR P FUJINON 90mm F22 1/30 EPR

94 Mr. Okazaki's Roji, "Around the Flagstones and Middle Gate", Present Age (Fukuoka)

The Okazaki family's garden has an audacious grouping of large stones at the foot of a mountain as well as a pond and a fountain to lead a stream. The roji is set under a grand cliff. The middle gate is located at the far end of the stepping stones. After passing it, one enters the garden of the Shunsui-an tea house. Such a plan reminiscent of Kyoto is outstanding.
SINAR P FUJINON 120mm F22 1/5 EPR

95 Mr. Tanakamaru's, "Flyfot Koshikake Waiting Bench", Present Age (Fukuoka)

The Tanakamaru's Residence is located on a hilltop in the city. The garden is composed mainly of lawns. Tea rooms and tea gardens are scattered in a part of the large mansion. The bower for waiting guests is an exact replica of the one at the Katsura Rikyu. The flyfot configuration of the bower was adopted to prevent noble guests from facing each other.
SINAR P SUPERANGULON 75mm F11 1/15 EPR

96 MOA's, "Golden Tea Ceremony Room A Complete View", Present Age (Shizuoka)

The idea to carry a ready-to-assemble tea house is interesting. Also building a tea room of gold is a fantastic plan. These ideas would not have come except for Hideyoshi. The tea room seems to have been located in the "honmaru" of Osaka Castle in the condition shown in this picture.
SINAR P NIKKOR 90mm F11 flash EPR

**齋藤忠一**

1939年、福島県に生まれる。東京芸術大学美術学部卒業後、作庭家重森三玲氏に師事。
興国寺庭園（和歌山）、凌雲寺庭園（愛知）、海泉寺庭園（神戸）、伊東マンダリンホテル庭園（静岡）、萩市役所庭園他多数作庭。
著書・共著に『探訪日本の庭』（小学館）『日本の庭園美』（集英社）『名園を歩く』（毎日新聞社）他多数。

Mr. Tadakazu Saito is a landscape gardener. He was born in Fukushima Prefecture in 1939. After graduating from Art Department of the Tokyo Art University, he studied under the direction of Mr. Mirei Shigemori. His works are the Kokoku-ji garden (Wakayama), the Ryoun-ji garden (Aichi), the Kaisen-ji garden (Kobe), Ito Mandarin Hotel garden (Shizuoka), Hagi-shi city hall garden and many others.
His books and joint works the "Tour of Japan Garden" (Shogakukan Publishing), "The beautiful Garden in Japan" (Shuei-sha Publishing), "Tour of Famous Garden" (Mainichi Newspapers) and many others.

# 露地の構成

日本庭園の中に、蹲踞を組み、飛び石を打ち、敷石や延段を舗き、灯篭を立てるようになったのは、すべては露地から発生した。

それは、理想とする山居の躰（佗び草庵の世界）を喧噪する街中の日常の生活空間の中に再現する手法として生まれ、発達した。

このような露地が創り出されたのは、桃山時代であるが、今日のごとく様式的に完成されたのは、江戸時代初期から中頃にかけてである。

こうして整った露地の基本は、まず露地口を潜って腰掛待合（外腰掛）に至る。

外腰掛は、招かれた客どうしの待合せ場所に相当する。腰掛には客数に応じて、正客石や次客石、連客石、お詰石などの役石が打たれる。役石の打ち方も茶人の好みによって、多様である。外腰掛には、実用のための下腹雪隠が付せられる。

亭主の迎付けを受けて、飛び石や敷石を踏んで中門に至る。中門は、茶人が理想とする山居の入口に当たり、迎付けは、客人を山居の柴門に出迎える、そういった心持ちの儀式である。

中門は佗びた風情を第一とする。屋根がなく、扉だけの門としては、猿戸、柴折戸、角柄戸、揚げ簀戸などがあり、屋根付きとしては、竹瓦葺門、萱葺門、檜皮葺門などがあり、形としては冠木門、四足門、腕木門、編笠などがある。屋根材や形の名称によった名前であるが、これらは、山居の躰に相応して設けられる。

中門の左右は、竹垣や生垣、植栽で仕切られる。この仕切りを間の垣という。

四ッ目垣、金閣寺垣、随流垣など透しの竹垣が一般的で、建仁寺垣、桂垣、大徳寺垣などの垣もある。

外腰掛から、この中門と間の垣までを外露地と呼ぶ。中門より中を内露地と呼ぶ。

飛び石を伝って蹲踞に至る。神仏に詣でる前に、清流や清浄水で手を洗い、口を漱ぐ。この洗手、漱口の清浄の思想が、清浄礼和を主旨とする茶道の根本精神に取り入れられて、蹲路や手水鉢として発達した。

亭主も客も、ともに蹲踞を使って心身を清めることによって、茶事が始まるとして、利休は、これを露地草庵の大本としたといわれる。

蹲踞は、手水鉢を低く据え、つくばって使うことからの名称であるが、その原風景は伊勢神宮に於ける御手洗川のごとく、清流につくばうイメージがある。理想とする山居がどのような所にあるかによって景趣が異なってくる。谷川の清流であったり、石清水であったり、大川であったり、湧き出る泉であったり、時には海であったりする。それによって、下り蹲踞となり、流れの手水となり、井戸蹲踞となる。

手水鉢が、自然石に水穴を穿ったものが最も多いのは、このように自然の景趣が根底にあるからである。

五輪塔や石塔などの石造品の残片を利用したものも用いられるようになり、さらには、まったく新しく創作されるようになった。

こうした蹲踞で心身を清めたのち、再び飛び石を伝って草庵の茶席に入る。途中、草庵の風情や扁額を賞しつつ進む。飛び石一つを進むごとに景趣が変化する。それが露地であり、飛び石の効用である。

飛び石は一歩たりとも歩む人の自由がない。飛び石の通りに客は進まなけれ

## Layout of "Roji"

Some features of the Japanese garden, the "tsukubai" (stone basin), "tobiishi" (stepping stones), "shikiishi" or "nobedan" (flagstones), and the "toro" (garden lanterns), were originated from the "roji" (the tea garden). These were created and nurtured as means of establishing a mountain hermitage, which is an ideal setting for the tea ceremony, in the din and bustle of the city where we spend our daily lives.

It was in the Momoyama Era (the late 16th century) when the "roji" was created as the backdrop for the "chanoyu". In the early and middle Edo Era (from the 17th to the 18th century), the garden of a tea house was definitely established as a style. The "roji" enhanced the profundity of the Japanese artistic practice of the ceremonial tea.

The basic layout of the "roji" leads guests to the "koshikake waiting bench", which is also called the "soto (outer) koshikake", through the "rojiguchi" (entrance to the "roji"). The "soto koshikake" provides visitors with a place to get together.

The host of the tea ceremony lays out keystones named the "shokyaku" (main guest) stone, "jikyaku" (No. 2 guest) stone, "renkyaku" (other guests) stone, and "otsume" (caretaker) stone according to the number of guests. The placement of the stones depends upon the preference of the ceremony master. There is a rest room ("shitabara setchin") nearby.

The guests proceed along the stepping stones and flagstones to the middle gate where the host welcomes them. This is called "mukae-tsuke". The "mukae-tsuke" reception at the middle gate derives from the idea that the host welcomes his visitors at the brushwood gate of his hermitage in the mountains. The middle gate, therefore, first and foremost must be of a simple and quiet appearance.

The design of the gate varies widely including the "sarudo" (wooden-plate door), "shiorido" (brushwood folding door), "tsunogarado" (wooden door with the ends of the head rail projecting), and "agesudo" (hanging door) as gates without roofs, and the "take kawarabuki" (bamboo tile roofing) gate, "kayabuki" (thatch-roofed) gate, and "hiwadabuki" (thatched with "hinoki" barks) gate as roofed gates. They can also be classified by design of the roof; that is, "kanmoto-mon" (a horizontal bar is placed between two gate posts), "shisoku-mon" (four-foot gate), "udegi-mon" (arm gate), and "amigasa" (braided hat gate).

They are named after the design of the door or roof and will be selected in accordance with the appearance of a tea house.

Bamboo fences, hedges or planting are built on both sides of the middle gate. This barrier is called "ai-no-gaki" (intermediate hedge). There is a wide variety of designs for the intermediate partition such as "yotsume-gaki" (lattice hedge), "Kinkaku-ji-gaki" (the Golden Pavilion hedge), and "zui-ryu-gaki" (a variation of lattice hedge). They are all openwork fences.

As solid fences, "Kenni-ji-gaki" "katsura-gaki" (bamboo hedge originated from the Katsura Imperial Villa), and "Daitoku-ji-gaki".

The area between the "soto koshikake" and the middle gate or the "ai-no-gaki" is called the "soto (outer) roji" and inside the gate is "uchi (inner) roji". The guest walks on the stepping stones from the middle gate to the "tsukubai". In the practice of Shintoism or Buddhism, people wash their hands and rinse their mouths with pure water or at a clean stream before worshipping gods or Buddha.

This act of hand washing and mouth rinsing was adapted as part of the principle of the tea ceremony which advocates "purity, manner and harmony", and manifested itself in the stone basin or the water basin.

It is said that Rikyu, the great master of "chanoyu", defined the stonework as the very center of the "roji" and tea house because the tea ceremony starts when the host and his guests wash their hands at the stone basin to purify their bodies and souls.

The word "tsukubai" comes from the word "tsuku bau" (to lean over) in reference to the fact that the stone basin is placed at a low position so that people must lean over to wash their hands. The "tsukubai" makes us imagine that worshippers purify themselves at a clear stream nearby called the "mitarashi-gawa" (river for hand washing) like the one at the Grand Shrine of Ise.

The imaginative setting of the mountain cottage or the tea house greatly affects the style of the "tsukubai". The stonework represents a mountain stream, a springwater, a big river, a fountain, or, sometimes, even the sea depending upon the plan of the tea house.

The style of the "tsukubai" will be also changed in accordance with the setting of the tea house and the "roji". Included in the style are the "ori (inclining) tsukubai", "nagare (stream) chozu", and "ido (well) tsukubai".

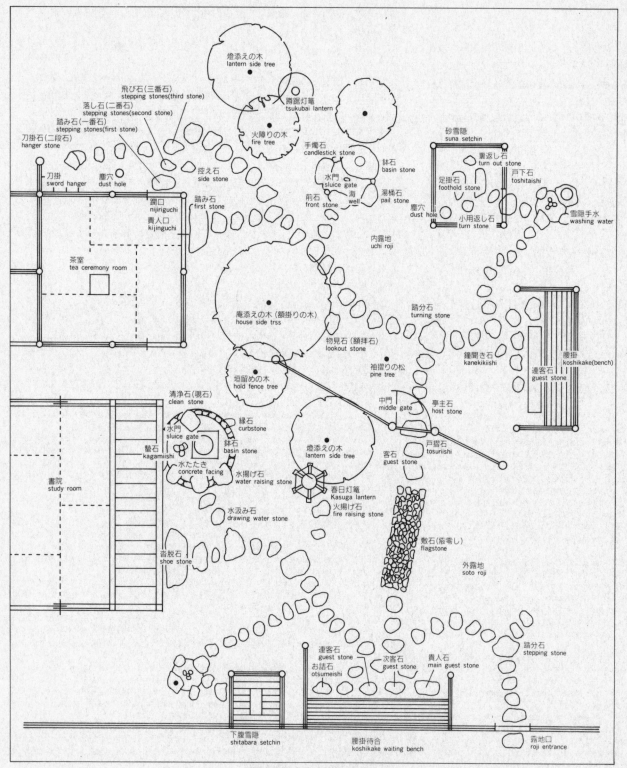

燈添えの木
lantern side tree

飛び石(三番石)
stepping stones(third stone)

蹲踞灯篭
tsukubai lantern

落し石(二番石)
stepping stones(second stone)

踏み石(一番石)
stepping stones(first stone)

火障りの木
fire tree

手燭石
candlestick stone

砂雪隠
suna setchin

裏返し石
turn out stone

刀掛石(二段石)
hanger stone

控え石
side stone

鉢石
basin stone

足掛石
foothold stone

戸下石
toshitaishi

刀掛
sword hanger

塵穴
dust hole

水門
sluice gate

湯桶石
pail stone

塵穴
dust hole

躙口
nijiriguchi

踏み石
first stone

前石
front stone

海
well

小用返し石
turn stone

雪隠手水
washing water

貴人口
kijinguchi

内露地
uchi roji

茶室
tea ceremony room

庵添えの木(額掛りの木)
house side trss

踏分石
turning stone

腰掛
koshikake(bench)

物見石(額拝石)
lookout stone

鐘聞き石
kanekikiishi

連客石
guest stone

袖摺りの松
pine tree

垣留めの木
hold fence tree

中門
middle gate

亭主石
host stone

清浄石(覗石)
clean stone

縁石
curbstone

戸摺石
tosuriishi

水門
sluice gate

鉢石
basin stone

客石
guest stone

蜆石
kagamiishi

水たたき
concrete facing

燈添えの木
lantern side tree

書院
study room

水揚げ石
water raising stone

春日灯篭
Kasuga lantern

水汲み石
drawing water stone

火揚げ石
fire raising stone

沓脱石
shoe stone

敷石(厳零し)
flagstone

外露地
soto roji

連客石
guest stone

踏分石
stepping stone

次客石
guest stone

貴人石
main guest stone

お詰石
otsumeishi

下腹雪隠
shitabara setchin

腰掛待合
koshikake waiting bench

露地口
roji entrance

露地役石名と会釈木の名称
A name of stepping stones and key trees in the Roji

ばならない。このことによって、客人の歩みのリズムや視線を規制して、こちらの理想とする景趣と感興に誘導することができる。

この飛び石について、利休は用を六分、景を四分としたのに対して、弟子の織部は用を四分に景を六分としたという。用と美の均衡の取り方を示して面白い。

露地全体は基本としては、この飛び石によってつながっており、それぞれの場所において、いろいろの働きを有しているものを役石と称している。

席入りをして懐石が終ると、席を改めるために客は中立ちする。そのときの休憩所として、内露地の中にも腰掛を設ける。作りは大体に外腰掛と同じであり、これを単に腰掛、あるいは内腰掛と呼んでいる。

内腰掛の付近には砂雪隠が設けられる。実際に使用することがないので飾雪隠とも称し、使用することはないが絶えず美しく掃除をしているので、中立ちのときには拝見する。

石灯篭は、露地の夜の路明りとして、神社や寺院の献灯用のものを応用したことにはじまる。石灯篭が立てられるポイントとしては、腰掛の辺り、中門の辺り、蹲踞の辺り、刀掛けの辺りを中心として、露地の長短や植栽の茂り具合、灯篭の大きさによって、いろいろと工夫される。

石灯篭は露地の景趣を非常に豊かにする。そのため、社寺のものを利用するだけでなく、茶人たちがそれぞれに好みに応じたものを作るようになった。中でも露地の佗びた風情を生かす方法として、台座石がなく、竿石をそのまま土中に埋め込んで立てる活け込み式の灯篭が多く用いられるようになった。織部灯篭などはその代表的なものである。

以上が最も一般的な露地で、この外露地、内露地の構成を二重露地と称している。この基本にいくつかの露地がつながって三重露地、多重露地となる。

露地口、外腰掛、下腹雪隠、中門、蹲踞、刀掛、塵穴、内腰掛、砂雪隠、石灯篭、井戸、茶席などの構成要素を結びつけるのが、飛び石や敷石であるが、そこに紅葉谷の景や、松林の景、樫林の景といった道すがらの山々の景色や山居の風情を表現するのが植栽である。

露地では、松一本が松林を表し、モミジ一株が深山の紅葉を表す。こうしたイメージの世界である。露地は非常に抽象的な世界である。

This idea underlies the fact that most of water basin are made of natural stones. Fragments of stoneworks such as five-story pagodas and "seki-to" stone towers began to supply materials for the water basin or "tsukubai" and then the production of original lanterns was started.

Purifying the body and soul, the guest takes a walk on the stepping stones to the tea house appreciating the atmosphere around the hermitage and a tablet hanging above the entrance. Every step of the guest will change views to the eye. This is the effect of the "roji" and the stepping stones.

The stepping stones do not allow the guest to walk at random. The walker must exactly trace the stones. Thus the host can control the rhythm of walking as well as the eye of the guest, and lead him to admire the landscape in the way the ceremony master intends.

Rikyu once defined the purpose of the stepping stones in the "roji" saying that 60 percent was for practical use and the rest for landscape admiration. However, Oribe, Rikyu's stepson, determined 60 percent for entertaining guests and 40 percent for practicality. It is very interesting to see the difference between the two big figures in the tea ceremony.

The "roji" is basically connected by the stepping stones. Some other stones at various points in the "roji" have their own purpose and are called "yakuishi" (keystones).

After having "kaiseki" (a meal served before the ceremonial tea), the guest once goes out of the tea house. This intermission is called "nakadachi."

To provide a place for waiting, another "koshikake" is nearby the tea house. This is simply called a "koshikake" or "uchi (inner) koshikake" in contrast with the "soto (outer) koshikake" in the "soto roji". The design is almost the same as that of the outer waiting spot.

Nearby the "uchi koshikake", a simple rest room named "suna setchin" (sand rest room) will be set up. However, this facility is never used and is thus dubbed the "kazari setchin" (false rest room). It is never used but kept clean and the guest is supposed to take a look during the intermission of "nakadachi".

Stone lanterns, "ishi-doro" or simply "toro" in Japanese, provide lighting to the "roji". In the early stages of ceremonial tea history, stone lanterns for Shinto shrines and Buddhist temples were used. Stone lanterns are usually placed near the "koshi-kake," the middle gate, "tsukubai", and "katanakake" (sword hanger). Howeever, they differ depending upon the size and shape of the "roji", plants and stone lanterns as well as at the host's discretion.

Stone lanterns enhance the interest of the "roji". Not only those for shrines and temples, but also original stone lanterns were designed and produced by tea ceremony masters. Such stone lanterns exclusively for the "roji" have no pedestal because simplicity is the essence of the tea ceremony.

In the tea garden, stone lanterns are placed with their "saoishi" (stem stone) directly inserted in the ground. This type of stone lantern (called "ikekomi" style) was employed more and more for the "roji". The "Oribe-doro" (a variation of stone lantern named after Oribe, Rikyu's stepson) is the most typical example of the "ikekomi" style.

This is a standard layout of the "roji" and the combination of the "soto roji" and the "uchi roji" is called the "niju(dual) roji". Adding another body of the "roji" to the basic arrangement of the "niju roji" makes variations of "sanju" (triple) and "taju (multiple) roji".

It is the stepping stones and flagstones which combine the components of the "roji" such as the "roji guchi" (entrance of the "roji"), "soto koshikake" (outer waiting bench), "shitabara setchin" (simple rest room at the "soto koshikake"), the middle gate, "tsukubai" "katana-kake" (sword hanger), "chiri-ana" (dust hole), "uchi koshikake" (inner waiting bench), "suna setchin" (simple rest room at the "uchikoshi-kake"), "ishi-doro (stone lantern), the well, and the tea house.

It is plants in the "roji" which reproduce scenary like a colored-leaf mountain, a black pine tree forest, or an evergreen oak forest depending upon the occasion or plan of a tea ceremony.

In the "roji", even a single black pine tree can represent a deep forest and a maple tree can stand for a mountain covered with colored leaves in autumn. This is the interpretation of items in the tea garden. The "roji" is a highly imaginative world.

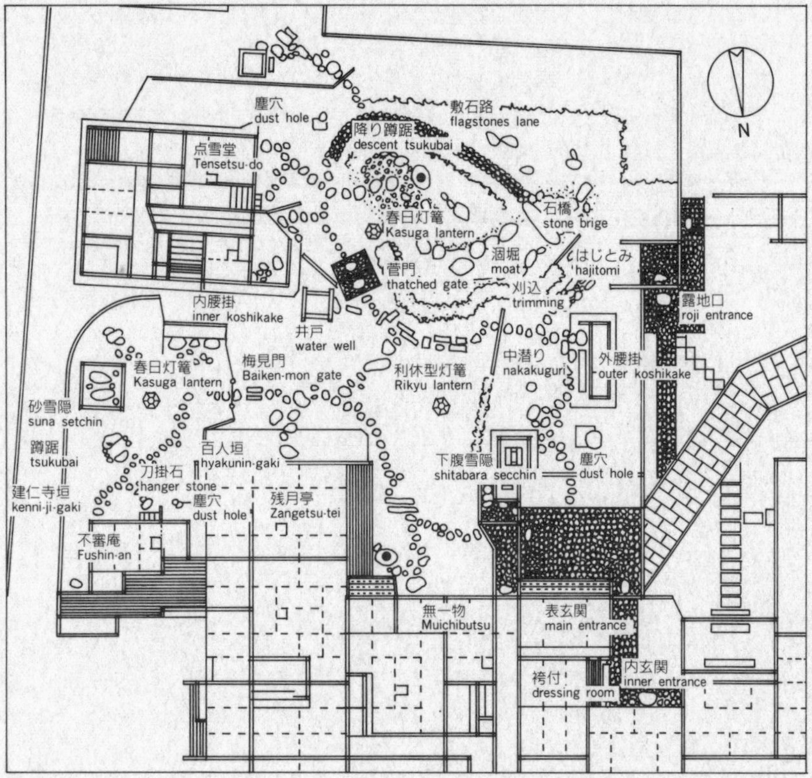

N
塵穴
dust hole
敷石路
flagstones lane
点雪堂
Tensetsu-do
降り蹲踞
descent tsukubai
春日灯籠
Kasuga lantern
石橋
stone brige
はじとみ
hajitomi
濠堀
moat
萱門
thatched gate
刈込
trimming
露地口
roji entrance
内腰掛
inner koshikake
井戸
water well
中潜り
nakakuguri
外腰掛
outer koshikake
春日灯籠
Kasuga lantern
梅見門
Baiken-mon gate
利休型灯籠
Rikyu lantern
砂雪隠
suna setchin
蹲踞
tsukubai
百人垣
hyakunin-gaki
刀掛石
hanger stone
下腹雪隠
shitabara secchin
塵穴
dust hole
建仁寺垣
kenni-ji-gaki
塵穴
dust hole
残月亭
Zangetsu-tei
不審庵
Fushin-an
無一物
Muichibutsu
表玄関
main entrance
内玄関
inner entrance
袴付
dressing room


## 表千家の露地 *(photo No.11▶ 14)*

露地口を潜って外腰掛に進む。正面に中潜りがある。不審庵へは、この中潜りで迎付けを受け、中潜りを潜って残月亭前の書院露地（中露地）を通り抜け、さらにもう一つの中門（梅見門）を潜って、不審庵前の内露地に至る。ここで蹲踞を使って席入りする。ここには、内腰掛と砂雪隠が設けられている。

外腰掛より右方へ飛び石と敷石を進んで揚げ簀戸を潜って点雪堂に至る露地がある。

揚げ簀戸を入ると枯流れに石橋が高く架っている。橋を渡って敷石道のゆるい坂をのぼる。峠に至って左にカーブをして点雪堂前に至る。左手に下りた枯流れの中に蹲踞が組まれている。麓で橋を渡った谷川の上流で手水をするイメージがある。鉢石は自然石で、流れの向うに据えられ、前石は流れの中にある。森閑として清冽な景趣である。

この露地では、揚げ簀戸を突きあげて、石橋をはさんで迎付けが行われる。亭主が峠を下って、谷川の麓の橋の所まで出迎えに来られる情景である。

山路の敷石は、山肌石を荒目に敷いて、山路の風情がよく感じられる。雨の後、山路の所々に砂利が洗われ出ている風情を面白く感じた利休が、露地の中に山路の景として移したといわれるが、非常にそのような感じの出ている道すがらである。

## Omote Senke's Roji *(photo No.11▶ 14)*

In the "roji" at the residence of the Omote Senke in Kyoto, you will pass through the entrance of the "roji" (roji-guchi) to the "soto koshikake" (outer waiting bench) where you will find a wicket gate named "nakakuguri" in front of you.

At the gate, the host will meet you and lead you to the "Fushin-an" tea house through the "nakaroji" (middle "roji") in front of a bower in the garden named the "Zangetsu-tei". You will go through another middle gate of "Baiken-mon" into the "uchi roji" (inner "roji") where you are supposed to wash your hands and mouth. The "uchi koshikake" and the "suna setchin" (simple rest room), which is never used, are there.

If you go to the right from the outer waiting spot, you will walk on stepping stones and flagstones until you reach another "roji" which is connected, through an "agesu-do" (hanging-door) gate, with the "Tensetsu-do".

Behind the hanging-door gate, there is the "kare nagare" (dry stream). A stone bridge crosses over the imaginative flow represented by stones. After walking over the stone bridge, you will climb a gentle slope covered with flagstones.

When you arrive at the peak of the ascent, you will turn left to get to the "Tensetsu-do". On your left is a "tsukubai" placed in the dry stream. This gives you an image that you wash your hands at the upper stream in the mountain of which you have crossed the lower stream at the foot of the mountain.

The basin is a natural stone and located on the other bank of the "kare nagare" while the "maeishi" (step stone of the "tsukubai") is in the imaginative flow. The effect is a clear, quiet place deep in the mountains.

In this particular "roji", the "mukae-tsuke" reception is conducted at the stone bridge over the dry stream. The idea is that, in order to welcome his guest, the host comes down along the pass from his mountain hermitage to the foot of the mountain where there is a small bridge over a clear stream.

Covering the mountain trail to the "Tensetsu-do" are rough pebbles which can effectively produce a deep-mountain atmosphere. It is said that Rikyu designed the path. When he found it interesting that the surface dirt had been washed away by rain and pebbles could be seen here and there on a mountain pass, he was so impressed that he decided to reproduce his impression in the "roji". Rikyu's aim is successfully reflected in the present layout.

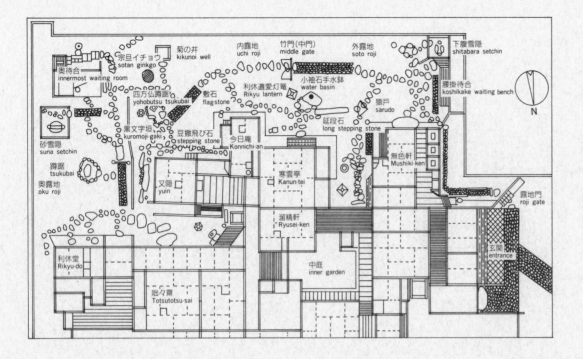

露地図（平面図）
（※図中の主な名称）
菊の井 kikunoi well
宗旦イチョウ sotan ginkgo
奥待合 innermost waiting room
四方仏蹲踞 yohobutsu tsukubai
敷石 flagstone
黒文字垣 kuromoji-gaki
砂雪隠 suna setchin
蹲踞 tsukubai
奥露地 oku roji
豆撒飛び石 stepping stone
又隠 yuin
利休堂 Rikyu-do
咄々齋 Totsutotsu-sai
内露地 uchi roji
竹門（中門） middle gate
利休遺愛灯籠 Rikyu lantern
今日庵 Konnichi-an
寒雲亭 Kanun-tei
溜精軒 Ryusei-ken
中庭 inner garden
外露地 soto roji
小袖石手水鉢 water basin
延段石 long stepping stone
猿戸 sarudo
無色軒 Mushiki-ken
下腹雪隠 shitabara setchin
腰掛待合 koshikake waiting bench
露地門 roji gate
玄関 entrance
N

## 裏千家の露地 （photo No.17▶20）

　外露地、内露地、奥露地の三重構成となっている。腰掛前で飛び石が二又に分れ、それが平行してほとんど真直ぐ奥へ進み、今日庵前で再び一緒になり、又隠前へと続く。

　外腰掛より左方の飛び石路を進むと猿戸だけの中門に至り、寒雲亭前に出る。猿戸の役石は石質や色彩を変え、そこから一枚の延石を末あがりに敷いてある。延石を渡り切った角に右斜めに蹲踞が組まれている。

　利休遺愛の小袖石の手水鉢で、表面が真平らで大きく、低く据えられている。濡れた蹲踞の景趣は、深い石清水を汲むがごとき感じがする。蹲踞は寒雲亭の右正面に組まれており、寒雲亭の庭ともなっている。

　蹲踞を使って、奥へ進むと今日庵の躙口となる。

　外腰掛より、右手の路を飛び石、敷石と真直ぐに進むと竹門に至る。二ツ割の竹を交互に合わせて葺いた門である。竹門を潜って飛び石を歩む。ほとんど直線的に打たれた飛石であるが、この辺りは非常に美しい。

　今日庵前よりの飛石と出合って、左方へ曲り、敷石に至る。敷石は右方へかすかに曲り、わずかに末あがりで非常に微妙な変化のある敷石である。

　敷石の端の右手に蹲踞がある。利休遺愛の四方仏の手水鉢である。

　蹲踞から又隠までの飛び石は、豆撒き飛び石といわれ、豆を撒いたように数多くの飛び石が打たれている。小振の飛び石を用に従って縦横に打ったもので、無作意といわれるが、実に計算された打ち方で、侘びた風情がある。

　又隠の東側は黒文字垣で仕切られ、利休堂前の奥露地がある。そこに奥待合があり、砂雪隠も設けられている。又隠より奥待合に行く途中に、菊の井があり、その脇に大きな宗旦イチョウが聳えている。

　奥露地には、揚げ簀戸の中門もあり、ここも二重露地の作りとなっている。

　灯篭は小袖の蹲踞、四方仏の蹲踞ともに活け込み式である。

## Urasenke's Roji （photo No.17▶20）

The "roji" of the Urasenke residence consists of three parts; "soto (outer)", "uchi (inner)" and "oku (innermost)" gardens.

Stepping stones separate into two directions at the "soto koshikake". The two trails of stones go in parallel to the "Konnichi-an" tea house and join together there connected to the "Yuin" (a room of the residence).

If you take the route to left from the "soto koshikake", you will reach the "Kanun-tei" (a bower in the garden) via a middle gate with a wooden-plate door (sarudo).

"Yakuishi" (keystones) at the "sarudo" gate are of various kinds and colors. One piece of the "nobeishi" (a long stepping stone) is placed from there. At the othe end of the "nobeishi", which is higher than the near end, there sits a "tsukubai."

This "tsukubai" is a relic of Rikyu and dubbed "Kosodeishi no chozubachi" (water basin of wadded silk garment stone).

Having washed your hands and rinsed your mouth at the "tsukubai", you will proceed onto the entrance of the "Konnichi-an".

If you take the other route to the right from the "soto koshikake", you will walk on the stepping stones and flagstones until you get to a bamboo gate ("take-mon").

At the point where the straight stepping stones meet another line of stones from the "Konnichi-an", you will have to turn right and find flagstones. The flags make a slight right curve and gradually ascend. If you carefully look at the flags, you will be able to appreciate the delicate and minute changes in their appearance.

A "tsukubai" is laid on the right edge of the stone path. This is another relic of Rikyu named "Yohobutsu no chozubachi" (water basin of the Buddha in the four direction. Stepping stones from the "tsukubai" to the "Yuin" are called the mame-maki" (bean-throwing) stepping stones. A large number of small stones are laid out like scattered beans. These "mamemaki" stepping stones are believed to have been invented by Sen Sotan.

The east side of the "Yuin" is separated by the "kuromoji-gaki" (spicebush hedge) constituting the "oku (innermost) roji" just in front of the "Rikyu-do" (Rikyu Hall). In the inner most "roji", there is the "oku machiai" (innermost waiting bench) with a "suna setchin" attached.

On the way from the "Yuin" to the "oku machiai", you will find a well named the "kikunoi" and next to the well there stands a gigantic gingko tree called the "Sotan Gingko Tree".

In the "oku roji", a middle gate in the "agesudo" style is placed so that the innermost garden of the Urasenke is of the "niju (dual) roji" type.

Stone lanterns in the area have no pedestal stones and their stem stones are directly standing on the ground. The "Kosode no chozubachi" and "Yohobutsu no chozubachi", relics of Rikyu are also of the same "ikekomi" style.

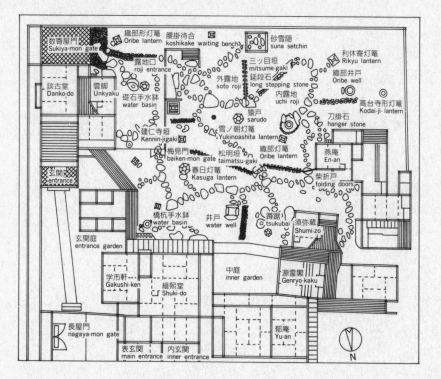

主要図内の各部名称：

織部形灯籠 Oribe lantern
数寄屋門 Sukiya-mon gate
腰掛待合 koshikake waiting bench
砂雪隠 suna setchin
利休寄灯籠 Rikyu lantern
談古堂 Danko-do
雲脚 Unkyaku
露地口 roji entrance
三ツ目垣 mitsume-gaki
外露地 soto roji
延段石 long stepping stone
織部井戸 Oribe well
礎石手水鉢 water basin
内露地 uchi roji
高台寺形灯籠 Kodai-ji lantern
建仁寺垣 Kennin-jigaki
猿戸 sarudo
刀掛石 hanger stone
雪ノ朝灯籠 Yukinoashita lantern
梅見門 baiken-mon gate
松明垣 taimatsu-gaki
織部灯籠 Oribe lantern
燕庵 En-an
玄関 entrance
春日灯籠 Kasuga lantern
柴折戸 folding doors
橋杭手水鉢 water basin
井戸 water well
蹲踞 tsukubai
須弥蔵 Shumi-zo
玄関庭 entrance garden
学市軒 Gakushi-ken
中庭 inner garden
絹煕堂 Shuki-do
源霊閣 Genryo-kaku
長屋門 nagaya-mon gate
表玄関 main entrance
内玄関 inner entrance
郁庵 Yu-an
N

## 藪内宗家の露地 *(photo No.28▶30)*

　燕庵は織部の京屋敷にあったものを初代剣仲が与えられて移築したもので、露地にも織部好みがよく現れている。その特色は貴人扱いの構成にある。

　露地口を入ると、潜り戸をはさんで鉤の手に両側に腰掛がある。左が貴人席で右が相伴席である。この形の腰掛を割腰掛と称している。

　貴人席の奥に離して砂雪隠があり、相伴席の横に続けて下腹雪隠がある。

　腰掛の前の大きな踏分石は、三つ小袖と称し、その向こうに袖摺松がある。

　三ツ小袖石の左右に猿戸がある。猿戸の戸摺石はわずかな段差ではあるが二段状の石で、迎付けのとき、貴人の場合は、その二段石の下の段に立って迎える。これも門前ではなく、ずっと途中まで出迎えることを意味する。貴人への御出迎えである。

　猿戸を入ると左方に斜めに振って、二間余の長さの延石を据え、片側に霰零しに耳石を敷き合わせている。佗びつつも華麗な延段である。利休の山路の敷石とはまったく趣を異にして、デザイン的でさえある。

　蹲踞は、文覚上人の五輪塔の水輪を鉢としたものといわれ、海をひとまわり大きくして、中央に据え、深く湧水を汲むような趣がある。

　前石は二人が並んで立てるほどに横長の大石を用いて、貴人の折には相伴者が手水を汲んでやれるように組まれている。

　灯籠は、猿戸横の雪の朝、延段突き当たりの利休の寄灯籠、織部井戸奥の高台寺型、蹲踞の織部形灯籠とすべてが活け込み式で、低く据えられている。

　この燕庵の二重露地を中心として、雲脚露地、絹煕堂の書院露地、須弥蔵の露地がつながって、全体としては非常に広い多重露地となっている。

## Yabunouchi Soke's Roji *(photo No.28▶30)*

The "En-an" was first built at the residence of Furuta Oribe in Kyoto and moved and reconstructed at the present site as it was given to the first Yabunouchi Kenchu, head of the Yabunouchi school. The "roji" around the tea house therefore reflects the preference of Oribe. The most remarkable point of the layout is its device for the nobility.

Entering the "roji guchi", you will find "koshikake" on both sides of the gate. The left "koshikake" is for noble people and the right for other participants ("shoban-seki"). This type of "koshikake" is called the "wari (split) koshikake".

The "suna setchin" is located away from the noble "koshikake" and the "shitabara setchin" is immediately next to the "koshikake" for commoners.

Just in front of the split "koshikake" is a big stepping stone named "Mitsukosode-ishi". You will find a black pine tree, the "Sodesuri matsu" across the stepping stone.

There is a "sarudo" gate to the left of the "Mitsukosodeishi". A stepping stone is placed under the gate. This particular stone has a step on its own surface. Though the height difference is very minute, it serves a clear-cut purpose. When the host welcomes a noble guest, he stands on the lower part of the stepping stone signifying that the host's place is not just in front of his gate but he comes a long way down to meet with his noble guest. Behind the "sarudo" gate, flagstones run diagonally to the left for about 3.6 meters and, to the right, a combination of "ararekoboshi" (pebbles in a uniform size) and the "mimiishi" (end stones of a stone step) are laid out on the ground.

Quite opposite to the mountain-path flags in the Omotesenke garden, the flagstones in the Yabunouchi garden have an artificial yet simple, quiet impression.

"Tsukubai" is believed that the basin was originally a part of the five-piece gravestone of Mongaku Shonin. At the center of the stone basin, a rather big hole was made so that you can enjoy as if you were scooping up water from a deep spring.

The step stone of the "tsukubai" is so wide that two people can stand on it at the same time. This is so a commoner can assist a noble guest in washing of the hands.

Several stone lanterns are placed in the garden such as the "Yukinoashita-doro" (stone lantern of the snow morning) near the "sarudo" gate, Rikyu's "Yose-doro" at the end of the flagstones, a Kodai-ji style lantern at the "Oribe-ido" (Oribe Well) and the "Oribe-doro" (Oribe lantern) at the "tsukubai". The stone lanterns are of the "ikekomi" style (having no pedestal), and they are all laid very low.

Centering around the dual "roji" of the "En-an", other "roji", such as the "Un-kyaku roji", "Shoin roji" at the "Shuki-do" (Shuki Hall) and the "roji" at the "Shumi-zo" (Shumi Warehouse) combine to constitute a "taju (multiple) roji".

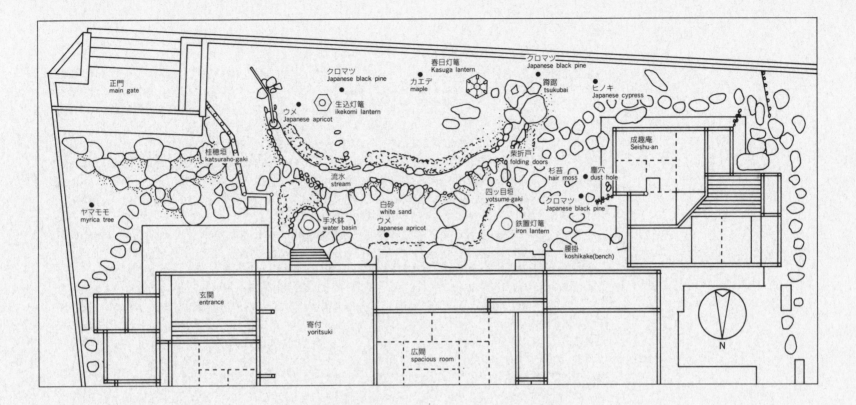

図中ラベル（plan labels）:

正門 main gate
クロマツ Japanese black pine
春日灯篭 Kasuga lantern
クロマツ Japanese black pine
ウメ Japanese apricot
生込灯篭 ikekomi lantern
カエデ maple
蹲踞 tsukubai
ヒノキ Japanese cypress
桂穂垣 katsuraho-gaki
柴折戸 folding doors
成趣庵 Seishu-an
ヤマモモ myrica tree
流水 stream
杉苔 hair moss
塵穴 dust hole
手水鉢 water basin
白砂 white sand
ウメ Japanese apricot
四ッ目垣 yotsume-gaki
クロマツ Japanese black pine
鉄置灯篭 iron lantern
腰掛 koshikake(bench)
玄関 entrance
寄付 yoritsuki
広間 spacious room
N

---

## 小堀宗家の露地 *(photo No.82▶ 83)*

　流れを中心とした二重露地である。寄附より、外露地に降りて、広間の前を東西に流れる小川に沿って飛び石を伝う。流れの手前は白砂を敷き、奥に軽い築山を築き、地苔を伏せて、モミジを植えている。この部分は広間から見ると書院の庭として見える。

　外露地に入るとすぐに中門の柴折戸と奥の茶室が、梅やモミジや松の間に見えがくれする。一歩進むごとに景趣が変化してくる。清流の河岸にある山居のイメージが感じられる。

　低い柴折戸を入った内露地は、一面が杉苔で、蹲踞は流れの端に組まれている。自然石を用いた雅趣のある蹲踞である。

　灯篭は活け込み灯篭、春日灯篭、鉄燈篭と明りに変化をもたせている。

　この露地は、東京信濃町にある遠州流家元の露地で、戦後の昭和二十九年に作庭された。

　大都市の中での現代生活の空間を考慮した露地である。

## Kobori Soke's Roji *(photo No.82▶ 83)*

The layout of the "roji" at the Kobori Soke residence is a dual "roji" centered around a stream.

You will go out to the "soto (outer) roji" from the waiting room (yoritsuki) and walk on the stepping stones along the stream which runs from east to west in front of a hall.

On the near side of the flow is scattered white sand while an artificial hill is built on the far side. Moss was planted and nurtured as well as maple trees.' If you look at the garden from the hall, it seems like a garden to the drawing room.

When you enter the "soto (outer) roji", the middle gate and the tea house are now visible and now invisible through the planting of Japanese apricot trees, maple trees and black pine trees. The view will change as you step forward. You can enjoy an image that you are walking to a mountain hermitage near a clear stream.

Inside the middle gate, the "uchi roji" is completely covered with moss, and a "tsukubai" was constructed at the stream. This "tsukubai" is made of natural stones and has a profound elegance in itself.

Several types of stone lanterns can be seen in the "roji" such as the "ikekomi-doro" (non-pedestal type lantern), and "tetsu-doro" (iron lantern on the stone). They provide a variety of lighting to the garden.

This "roji" is located at the residence of the head of the Enshu school in Shinano-machi, Tokyo. The garden was built in 1954, after World War II. The design of the "roji" reflects consideration of an urban, modern lifestyle.

## あとがき

　私は、茶事のことについてはほとんど知らないといっていい。

　茶室、露地については相当数のものは拝見させて頂いたり、撮影させて頂いてきた。露地や茶室を写真に撮影させて頂くとき、茶事のことをよく知っていて、撮影することのほうがいい写真になることは当然のことであろう。というのは露地の庭くらい約束事、定まりの多い庭はないということである。それは普通の庭園のように庭そのものを鑑賞的に、立ったり座ったりして眺めるものではないということである。

　露地、茶室の庭は、お茶を飲むための前座、セレモニーといった要素が非常に強くある。そこにはお茶を通して接待する側の亭主と、接待される側の客がいなくてはならない。亭主は自分で露地を掃き清め、飛び石や、敷石、植栽に打ち水をし、塵を払い、手水鉢に清水を汲み入れ、客を待つ。

　客は客で決められた時間に、露地門から入庭し待合に集合して入室の合図を待つ、ここらあたりから露地の茶事が始まるのである。多くの茶人の心ときめく瞬間である。

　ゆるい登り勾配の敷石は深い山道の景、両側の緑の植栽は林立する木立の景色である、峨々たる渓谷には橋がかかっている、細い流れは深い谷なのである。飛び石伝いの道は鄙びた野道、道すがらの景色だ。

　客は、一椀のお茶を喫するため、遠く野を越え、山を越え谷を越えて辿り着くといった設定なのである。

　中門は亭主と客がこの露地の中で一番初めに出会う所である。初めて顔を見合わせ挨拶をかわすための役石がしつらえられてある。ここからを内露地という、一種の結界である。先ほどの待合腰掛付近を外露地とよぶのであるがこの形式が二重、三重に作られている露地もある。

　内露地にはその茶室の歴史や伝統が多く隠されている。裏千家の露地でいうと、利休遺愛の小袖の手水鉢、利休遺愛の灯篭、利休遺愛の四方仏蹲踞、宗旦イチョウといった風にである。このほか敷石、飛び石、額見石、刀掛石、井筒、踏分石、塵穴、貴人石等、役石だらけである。これらの役石や定まりをいかに自然に、間違ってもいいから、自分の心得の中で使いこなすことが、心を込めた亭主の気持ちに答える客の礼儀であろう。露地というものはそういうものであろうと私は思う。

　私は今まで、一般の庭園というものをたくさん撮影させて頂いてきたが、露地、茶庭そのものを集中的に撮影し拝見させてもらったのは今回が初めてでしかも写真集にしようと思っている。自分ながら大変なことをしている、という思いがする。私の庭園の師匠今は亡き重森三玲先生はことのほか茶事がお好きであった。新年の初釜やなにか茶事があると必ずお招きを頂いていたが、どうしても好きになれずあまり出席をしなかったが、今になって思えばもったいないことをしたと悔んでいる。あのとき勉強しておけばもっといい写真が撮れたのでは……。

　先生は口癖のように君には君のお茶があるのだから、君の勝手に飲めばよろしい、肝心なのは亭主に失礼のないよう、美しく飲むことだとおっしゃっていた。この形は喫茶には大事な教えだと思う。あるとき先生の茶室に通されたことがあった。大きな笑い声が聞えてきていかにも楽しそうな雰囲気が漂っていて、小柄なお坊さんが薄ごろもを着、大あぐらをかいて座っておられる。しかも夏のことであったのでもろ肌が見えているのだが、これがまたいやらしくなく自然体なのだ、実に夏の茶会らしく涼しげで豪快で飲んでおられる作法も美しい。これだな、と、思った。先生は無言のうちに、私にお茶のなんたるかを教えていてくれたのだ。今でもその光景は鮮明に頭の中に残っている。そのお坊さんが有名な大徳寺の和尚、立花大亀老師だということを後で聞いて驚いた。利休は、創作々々を続けて草庵の侘茶を完成させた。長い伝統の中で新しいことをするのにはいつの世でも抵抗と困難がつきまとう。利休はそれを乗り越えたそれが偉大なのだ。昔にあったものが今の新しい露地にはないものがある、それも仕方がなくこれからの露地、茶庭も変貌していくであろうが、この小冊子が古典露地茶庭の記録としてなにかのお役に立てるとすればこんなうれしいことはないと同時に、その期待に添えるか心配である。

　諸兄のご高評を賜りたいと思う。終りに裏千家お家元、千宗室宗匠に序文を頂戴し心から厚く御礼を申し上げます。ありがとうございました。

　最後に、茶庭の解説、資料を提供して頂いた齋藤忠一氏、再三再四にわたるこの本の企画、進行を担当してくれたグラフィック社の赤平覚三氏、デザイナーの熊谷博人氏、私の仕事を終生見つめていてくれる重森弘淹氏の方々に心を込めて御礼申し上げますとともに、地下に眠られている三玲先生に再度見てほしいと思っている。

1989年10月

大 橋 治 三

# AFTERWORD

It is probably safe to say that I in fact know very little about matters relating to tea.

I have seen a considerable amount of tea rooms and roji and taken many photographs of them. Of course, when one does dedicate a great deal of time to taking photographs of tea rooms and roji a workable knowledge of the world of tea would help to improve the quality of each picture. In other words, there is no other style of garden that has so many conventions and regulations as the roji garden. This means that one does not just sit and enjoy a roji garden as one would an ordinary garden.

The roji or tea garden contains strong elements of the tea ceremony and acts as the opening curtain to the actual process of drinking the tea. The host and the guest play the essential roles in this play. The host sweeps the garden, sprinkles water onto the stepping stones, flagstones and plants, shakes off any accumulated dust, fills the water basin with spring water and then awaits the guest.

The guests are expected to enter from the roji gate punctualy and sit on the waiting bench until their names are called. It is only after these formalities are complete that the actual drinking of tea can commence.

It is at this moment that many tea-masters feel the thrill of pride.

The gently sloped flagstones represent a view of a deep mountain path. The green plants on either side are the forest. A bridge fords the rugged valley; represented by the thin brook. The path alongside the stepping stones is likened to an ageless rustic track.

The appeal of the garden to the guest is suggestive of having struggled over rough seas, steep mountains and deep valleys in order to obtain a bowl of tea.

The middle gate is the place that the host and the guest will meet for the first time. The place where this meeting must take place is carefully marked out by the Yakuishi (keystone). From here on the roji becomes known as the uchi (inner) roji; as if it were a border. The location of the Koshikake waiting bench is in the soto (outer) roji. Some roji repeat this layout two or three times. The traditions and history of the tea room is contained within the uchi-roji. The Urasanke roji contains the water basin treasured by Rikyu, a Rikyu lantern, a Rikyu Yohobutsu tsukubai and a Sotan gingko tree. In addition to this, the roji is crammed with yakuishi, flagstones, stepping stones, lookout stones, hanger stones, a well, a dust hole and kijinishi, etc. It is considered social etiquette for the guest to respond to the heartfelt hospitality of the host by acting the role of honoured guest as naturally as possible within the limits of one's knowledge and understanding. It is my personal opinion that mistakes will be tolerated without problem if the guest is willing to enter into the spirit of the ceremony.

I have taken many photographs of ordinary gardens throughout my career, but this is the first time that I have focused my lens on the tea garden and the successful result has decided me to turn the end product into a book. This seems to me to be a very responsible thing to do. The late Mirei Shigemori, my garden master, used to like the tea ceremony more than anything. Many is the time that he invited me to participate in his ceremonies at the time of New Year and other special occasions, but I seldom accepted the invitations owing to a difficulty on my part to appreciate the grandeur of the occasion. This is now my deepest regret. I wish I had studied it when I was filled with a youthful sense of humility. Maybe then I would have been better qualified to take photographs of tea gardens. He used to tell me to drink the tea anyway in which I wished as all people have their own interpretation of the ceremony and the most important thing is to drink with beauty and avoid offending the host. This has remained an important lesson for me. On one occasion he led me to his tea room and from within came the sound of loud and raucous laughter. There sat a small Buddhist priest dressed in a robe and filled with a happy mood. He was sitting cross-legged, and owing to the heat of the summer his chest and arms were bare. However, this style looked natural rather than indecent and was certainly suited to the hot summer. The way in which he was drinking the tea was exciting and beautiful. It was then that I understood the import of the master's lesson, and he had managed to make me understand by using the large-hearted priest as a case-study. This sight still remains vividly within my head, and I was later suprised to discover that the priest was in fact Daiki Tachibana, the priest of Daitoku-ji temple.

Rikyu completed the "wabicha" hermitage after repeating many creations. It is impossible to avoid critisism and opposition when something new breaks age-old traditions. This is as true today as it was centuries ago. Rikyu overcame this opposition which in itself is equal to a great work. There are therefore some things which cannot be seen in modern roji gradens. This cannot be helped. Futher roji gardens will also experience change. I would be more than happy if this book comes in useful as a reference to ancient roji gardens, but I must admit a little trepidation as to whether it is worthy of this role. I would be more than grateful to receive your esteemed opinions on this point. I would also like to take this oportunity to offer my thanks to Sen Soshitsu, the head of Urasenke.

I would also like to express my gratitude to Mr. Tadakazu Saito who provided me with commentary and information on tea gardens, to Kakuzo Akahira of Graphic-Sha Publishing who took charge of the planning and processing of the book, to Hiroto Kumagai the designer, and to Koen Shigemori who closely monitored my work. I would also like to express a desire for Mr. Mirei, who is now resting in peace, to be able to see this work.

October 1989

Haruzo Ohashi

## 大橋治三略歴

1927 ● 大阪市に生まれる。棚橋紫水氏に師事する
1957 ● 上京後フリーの写真家となる
1969 ●《日本の名園》(誠文堂新光社)
1973 ●《湖国近江》(毎日新聞社)
1976 ●《日本庭園史大系(全35巻)》(社会思想社)
1977 ●《日本庭園手法集(全5巻)》(毎日新聞社)
1980 ●《面打ち長沢氏春氏》(毎日新聞社)
1984 ●《古能面傑作集50選》(毎日新聞社)
　　　●《修学院離宮》(新潮社)
1986 ●《四季日本の庭》(グラフィック社)
　　　●《続四季日本の庭》(グラフィック社)
1987 ●《坪庭》(グラフィック社)
1989 ●《名園を歩く(全8巻)》(毎日新聞社)
　　　●《大仙院》(集英社)他多数
　　　●現在、日本写真家協会・二科会会員
現住所●〒350-13 狭山市北入曽829-15 TEL.(0429)58-6567

*The Tea Garden*　　photographed by Haruzo Ohashi

## 茶庭　大橋治三写真集

1989年11月25日 ● 初版第1刷発行


著　者●大橋治三ⓒ
発行者●久世利郎
印刷所●凸版印刷株式会社
製本所●和田製本株式会社
写　植●株式会社三山綜合システム
発行所●株式会社グラフィック社
　　　　〒102 東京都千代田区九段北1-9-12
　　　　電話03・263・4318 振替・東京3-114345
　　　　落丁・乱丁本はお取替え致します。
ISBN4-7661-0543-5 C0072